THE RACIAL MYTH

THE
RACIAL MYTH

BY
PAUL RADIN

Author of "Social Anthropology" and
"Primitive Man as Philosopher"

WHITTLESEY HOUSE
McGRAW-HILL BOOK COMPANY, INC.

NEW YORK · 1934

Published by

WHITTLESEY HOUSE

A Division of the
McGraw-Hill Book Company, Inc.

Printed in the United States of America by
The Maple Press Company, York, Pa.

TO THE MEMORY OF MY FATHER

Who was always in the vanguard of liberal movements and who understood, as he exemplified in his life, the dictum of the great Greek:

'Tis not in hate, but love, that men unite themselves.

PERHAPS no event of recent times has provoked more astonishment and incredulity than the assertion lately put forward that specific peoples belong to a superior race and that everything great and significant in the history of the world has been accomplished by them. Since we are ostensibly dealing here with mature people it is necessary to take cognizance of their claims. Fortunately we need not enter into any polemics with them. The facts speak for themselves. It is in an attempt to state what these facts are and how it has come about that race and nationality lend themselves so easily to misinterpretation and abuse that the following book has been written.

In the crisis of civilization through which we are now passing, no thinking and feeling man can long remain untouched and unaffected. For that reason a brief review of the history of civilization and the contributions of the various races, mixed and unmixed, may possibly be of service and value. Such a survey indicates quite clearly that all specific racial pretensions to superiority are both illusory and unjustified.

CONTENTS

PAGE

FOREWORD 3

CHAPTER I

THE MYTH OF RACIAL SUPERIORITY THROUGH THE
AGES. 5

CHAPTER II

THE ILLUSION OF THE CONFUSED LATE COMERS:
THE NORDIC MYTH 19

CHAPTER III

THE TORCH OF CIVILIZATION: FROM THE STONE AGE
TO TODAY. 52

CHAPTER IV

THE EUROPEAN ACHIEVEMENT SINCE THE SIXTEENTH
CENTURY: THE NEW INSTRUMENT AND THE NEW
NATIONALISM 73

CHAPTER V

THE PAN-EUROPEAN ACHIEVEMENT IN THE NINE-
TEENTH CENTURY: THE NEW ART OF THOUGHT 94

CHAPTER VI

THE CONFEDERATION OF THE WORLD 121

THE RACIAL MYTH

FOREWORD

THE end of an economic order and a whole system of thought is so palpably upon us today that we should perhaps be tolerant of orgies that spring from desperation and ignorance that is simple ignorance, and lack of understanding. But those of us who have preserved some vestige of intellectual and emotional poise cannot forget the gamut history runs; we cannot forget that, at such times, man tends to take refuge with the monsters and dragons infesting the pool of his unconscious and unanchored self; that, at such times, he refuses to be, or possibly cannot be, intelligently rational. So he returns to an imaginary past, rendered doubly dishonest and contemptible because it is a confession of inability and unwillingness to live in the present. The description of this past in the mouths of grown-up individuals cannot be so unconscious and free from wicked and willful distortion as they pretend it to be.

It is possibly because protests in the past generations have been too few or in the wrong manner, possibly because intellectual protests are never efficacious in a world of action, that they have had no influence. Still these protests must be made. It is because there are not enough of them that history repeats itself, and history need not repeat itself. There is nothing inherent in cultural change that demands this. We cannot, therefore, look with unconcern when one of the bearers of modern civilization deliberately turns her back upon her true past, to summon back the tenuous ghosts of her untutored ancestors.

Yet how can we meet the menace? It is not simply that ghosts are easier to summon than to exorcise; it is that ghosts are dangerous to all of us, the bystanders as well as the summoners. The world, unfortunately, has always been tolerant of them. But of one thing ghosts have always been afraid, of the light. Even if those in question have developed a certain degree of immunity to the direct rays of the sun, still they will shiver and grow cold when exposed to it.

The only pertinent and correct answer to a bloodshot mirage is a presentation of the actual facts, so that the innocent spectator may become aware that he is in the presence of an illusion. In its broad outlines the history of mankind is fairly well-known today. We know what the milestones were and we know the physical type of those connected with these milestones. That is what I propose to give here.

If, at times, it is essential to become indignant, it is not at people, but at the existence of sophisticated ignorance, for this is not merely harmful in itself but an insult to that small and precarious margin of improvement which separates man from the apes.

CHAPTER I

THE MYTH OF RACIAL SUPERIORITY THROUGH THE AGES

The history of civilization is largely the account of the attempts of man to forget himself. Small wonder that he should. It is, after all, only a comparatively short time since he has, in his reactions, become sufficiently differentiated from the manlike apes for anyone of more than normal sensibilities always to distinguish accurately between the two. The untoward accident that gave him the new and specifically integrated nervous system which we call human and added an upright posture brought its full quota of woe and misery into this world. In all fairness, with his new nervous equipment, there should have come a new outward frame. But nature willed it otherwise. Instead, she allowed him merely a change from a horizontal posture to an upright one. Thus his frame belied his brain or, at least, that part of his brain which was new and, as the contrast and the incongruity between them slowly dawned upon him, he grew fretful and somewhat justifiably resentful. What answer, indeed, was he to find to the perplexing problems that suddenly crowded upon him as he realized with ever-increasing poignancy that his motor reactions and his emotions were predominantly animal and only his thinking was human? Certainly, at the beginning there could have been nothing but bewilderment illumined by doubt.

Nor did the struggle for existence and the ensuing revelation of his animal-human nature add to his comfort or assuage his newly acquired fears. To orient himself in a world neither of his making nor of his choosing he invented God; to gain even a measure of peace he took solace in dreams. And the first dream with which he seems to have played and to have elaborated was that of a time in the not too distant past where there had been no strife inward or outward: a Golden Age which would, indeed, return again in the not too distant future, where nothing of the animal would cling to him and the highest aspirations of his thought and the outpourings of his purified emotions would find clear and unhampered expression.

The records of all people, primitive and civilized, begin with this dream of a Golden Age where people never grow up or where they rest after the strain of their earthly experience. Originally, certainly, this

6

was a democratic realm in which no distinctions, racial or national, existed. Manifestly its main purpose was to forget reality, to forget the conflict of the animal human being with the human animal as he slowly and inconsistently sloughed off his pristine heritage. But life was too much upon him. It seemed to confirm his most pessimistic forebodings about the apparent wickedness of the human heart, about the unchangeability of human nature, and to pollute his thought at the very fountainhead. Realities obtruded themselves upon him everywhere and reechoed unpleasantly even in that one dream which he had sought to keep free from life's enveloping egotism. The Golden Age thus became tarnished and in an apparent effort to save it man confusedly pushed it ever farther away from him, into the past. But he never forgot it, never ceased speculating upon why it had disappeared and when it would return again. Romanticists like the ancient Egyptians put it to comparatively little use. But those stubborn realists the Semites, more particularly the Hebrews, found in its symbolism a much desired refuge. By that time, however, this glamorous dream had become completely saturated with the smell of the world, had become simply an aureoled mirror of a specific earthly order, the Semitic world of 800 B.C.

Doubtless this had happened before, among countless peoples, but the peculiar enmeshment of the realities of life with an old compensation dream received its first significant expression among these early Hebrews maintaining a militant and precarious existence in a country open and exposed to attack on all sides. That they should have survived at all was an achievement of which they could well be proud; that they should have succeeded in welding the disparate elements of their civilization into a new and specific unity, with a quality all its own, was almost a miracle. As such they regarded it. For them it became a proof that God had intervened in their behalf, that they were the elect of the Deity, a chosen nation. The peoples around them, alien in blood and speech, were not merely different, but the rejected of the Lord. If, however, they were superior to the rest of mankind, it was not by virtue of any inherent racial trait, nor because of their outstanding gifts, but because they possessed the one prime virtue—that of obeying the Lord's commandments.

The Jews were thus well launched on a program that must inevitably have led to a belief in their national and racial superiority when the thunders of the Prophets and the vicissitudes of war frustrated them. Defeat, captivity, and insecurity forced upon them a revision of the old dream. It was no longer the yearning for the return of a Golden Age but the yearning for a haven of rest, for the coming of a Messiah who would usher in a new order of values. They could still glory in their title of the Chosen People and cling to the memory of their transitory victories and national independence but, fortunately, there could be no further strengthening of that illusion, born of a dream and of human egotism, that they were inherently a superior race or a superior nation. After the destruction of the Temple by Titus in A.D. 70 and their final dispersion, the Jews developed a strong racial pride which possessed many of the characteristics of a belief in racial superiority. But here again the economic and cultural function fate bestowed upon them came to their rescue.

For the Jewish formula, the elect of God as opposed to the rejected of God, the Greeks substituted the children of light as opposed to the barbarians. In this they were at one with the vast majority of peoples. For most tribes and nations the contrast has always been between those who are in and those who are out, those who speak your language and those who speak a different one, those who possess your virtues and vices and those who have alien virtues and vices. From the beginning of time the members of one group have always regarded it as something of an impertinence not unmixed with the ridiculous that other groups should converse in accents that had no meaning for them or sin in a fashion unknown among themselves. The Greeks were the first to formulate this opposition, so dear to the human heart, and they have left us in the word "barbarian," *i.e.*, the strange, the uncouth, the whole epitome of racial contrasts and racial evaluations.

If the Greeks developed no marked feeling of racial superiority, the reason is to be sought in the simple fact that for them other people did not exist, so that there was no need for despising them and manifestly little need for emphasizing their own importance. It remained for that part of Greece that had but recently identified itself with the true Greek tradition and culture, Macedonia, to produce the man who prided himself upon being a Greek and who sought to demonstrate Greek superiority by conquering the world. He conquered the world and proved Greek superiority, but at the fortunate price of including under the designation Greece all those who adopted the Greek language as their mother tongue and Greek culture as the frame in which to work out their individual destinies. Obviously there was no room here for any theory of inherent racial traits or for a doctrine of Greek superiority, since the world that mattered was Greek.

While Alexander the Great was spreading Greek culture over the Orient and creating a pannationalist if not an internationalist civilization, a small and stubborn people were slowly emerging from obscurity on the Italic peninsula who were, for a time, at least, to preach the doctrine that racial purity was a merit in itself and that national superiority was a fact that the conquered and the inferior peoples of the earth should duly recognize and pay homage to. The civilization of Latium and its capital

10

Rome was the ideal soil for such a theory. A farming people of homely virtues, surrounded by an opulent Greek civilization on the south and a virile and integrated Etruscan culture on the north, who within a period of two centuries succeeded in conquering and dominating Italy from Etruria to Apulia and from the Tyrrhenian Sea to the Adriatic, and who yet remained fundamentally untouched, might well interpret their victory as due to having remained untouched and justifiably extol those traits in their character in which they differed from their luxurious neighbors.

These traits, the Romans insisted, were a racial stock with little if any foreign admixture, frugality, simplicity, courage, and the power of enduring hardships. Clearly these were the virtues of husbandmen and warriors, of realists close to the soil and none too quick in their mental reactions. Like true peasants, they hated the refinements of civilization as long as they knew nothing about them and succumbed to them with voracious alacrity as soon as they were introduced. The conquest of Greece (146 B.C.) and the close contact with the Hellenistic Orient brought these refinements to Rome, and after that the purists and the jingo politicians could preach and rant to their hearts' content about the simple virtues that had supposedly led to the Roman victory over their rich and supercultured neighbors; the Romans themselves preferred to forget them. The insistence upon

11

racial purity had been abandoned long before. Significantly enough, it had developed not so much from the dislike of Romans to intermarry with foreigners as from the unwillingness of the Roman patricians to intermarry with the Roman freedmen. When that conflict ceased, the doctrine of caste and racial purity lost most of its meaning and became merged in the much larger thesis of the superiority of being a Roman citizen.

Yet, as so often happens whenever the semblance of democracy and rusticity has gone, the poets and intellectuals looked back with sentimental enlargement upon their rural past and combined it with the Latin version of the myth of the Golden Age. For the greatest poet of them all—Virgil—there was to be no return to pristine hardship and frugality. Even if, as he says, "some stains of the old-time sin live on, to bid man tempt the sea in ships, girdle his towns with walls, cleave his furrows in the soil," still the new age was upon them. A better race is to displace our own and in the new realm all that will be required of man is that he know virtue and, recognizing it, watch, hour by hour, the fields grow more yellow with ripening corn, the grapes hang on the uncouth bramble, the oak drip with honey-dew, and mankind be as one.

Thus confusedly and inconsistently did the Romans pass from racial to national arrogance and end in a poet's dream of universal brotherhood. Like the Greeks, the lure for domination and empire had at least this saving grace: it destroyed the essential basis for the illusion that one particular race or one particular people were superlatively and inherently endowed.

Roman nationalism as such ceased to have any significant ethnical meaning after Caracalla declared all people living within the Roman Empire Roman citizens and received its final death thrust when, in the fourth century A.D., it was overwhelmed by early Christian universalism and the doctrine, derived from the Jewish prophets, that all peoples were as one within the loving kindness of God, if they but accepted Him.

By the seventh century Christianity reigned supreme over most parts of the old Roman Empire, and racial and national designations were rendered secondary in importance to religious ones. Faith thus cut across biological and cultural barriers. An Italian, Spanish, or French Catholic, heir of the Roman tradition and culture, was as one with the unmannered British or the mead-drinking German Catholic, still bewildered and befuddled from the intoxicating contact with a mature and complex culture. Any theory of racial purity had, of course, no place here.

But if the doctrine of national superiority was, to all intents, excluded, that did not imply that peoples had suddenly lost their ineradicable urge for designating the beliefs they held as inherently true, proper, and altogether superior and contrary faiths

13

as viciously and ludicrously false, improper, and inferior. For Christianity the characteristics of superiority were thus two: the genuine belief in certain dogmas and the recognition of the supremacy of the Church. The unbeliever was not only exterminated in this world but he was eternally damned in the next. Yet since it opened its portals wide to receive the unbeliever as soon as he saw the true light, and welcomed the heretic back to the fold with redoubled joy, even the drastic and ferocious treatment it meted out to nonbelievers can almost be condoned in view of the Church's universal character and the fact that for so many years it held in check the wild forces of nationalism.

From the fifth century to the sixteenth, in spite of all the economic and political factors opposing the simple declaration that you are saved by faith and rendered superior by faith whatsoever be your language, specific country, head form, or skin color, the Church adhered steadfastly to this one doctrine. With the development of the unified and well-knit kingdoms of France, England, and Spain in the fifteenth century, the fate of universalism was, for the time being at least, sealed, and we have the tale of Macedonia and early Rome partially repeated—small peoples on the margin of a great culture coming into their own and setting out to conquer or dominate the neighboring world. But there was this difference. France, England, and Spain set out on their task at approximately the

14

same time, whereas Rome had no equally powerful competition nor was there, for a long time, a land that could play for them the rôle Greece and Asia Minor played for Rome.

In the struggle for supremacy that began in the sixteenth century in Europe, each country was, in characteristic fashion, led to interpret the traits that presumably gave it a temporary victory as the earmarks of superiority. Aided and abetted by poets and professors, a formidable list of specific national virtues was drawn up which were supposed to have held true from the beginning of their history and to have found expression in every phase of their life.

The sanguinary cruelty of Castile and Aragon, easily enough explicable when we remember the ceaseless battle they waged against the Arab invaders of Spain for seven hundred years, was reinterpreted as the stern, uncompromising valor and faith of a disinherited people struggling to regain its patrimony. The natural and possibly inevitable tendency for a people, after a hard-won victory stretching over centuries, to exclude from all participation in their government those against whom they had fought so long, and to pride themselves that no blood of their hated enemies, Arabs and Jews, flowed in their veins, was interpreted as a proud consciousness of their racial purity.

Similarly, the set of manners connected with those highly formalized games the tournaments

15

and the courts of love of the thirteenth and fourteenth centuries, which bore no relation to the general level of manners even of the small minority who
participated in them, was accepted as evidence of
the innate French feeling for courtesy, of their
ineradicable sense of honor, of their love of form.
With this was coupled the theory that the French
have instinctively always expressed themselves
with crystal clarity and that they represented the
epitome of rationality.

The English, on the other hand, because their
soldiers and traders conducted themselves with a
stubborn courage and a reckless fear of conse-
quences, born of the fact that they had no set and
accepted standard of behavior to which to conform,
were credited with an inborn resistance to formalized patterns and a rugged individualism that
brooked no control. They were sung and extolled as
a people who were ready to sacrifice their all in the
defense of personal liberty.

The Italians were to attain no unification largely
because of these northern harassers. And although
her poets might lament Italia's possession of that
unhappy gift of beauty which made her the lure for
the lustful ill-mannered foreigner and brought
unmerited destruction upon her, yet this apparent
tragedy has also meant that she remained civilized
and free from the dangerous sentimentalism of
the newly unified nations. When the Italians finally
attained their unity, in our own time, the period had
16

passed for Italy, at least, where a poet's slogans were to have great validity.

Unhappy Germany, always on the periphery of the great movements that swept over Europe, was to wait till far into the nineteenth century to attain unity, even of a kind. But unfortunately the type of unity she achieved was then definitely on the wane and making place for a newer and truer integration, on economic foundations. Thus her interpretation of why she had won and what characteristics in her people had made her victory possible, which in no wise differed from the assessments Spain, France, and England had made before her, sounded strange in the ears of the business civilizations of Europe. Nor was this strangeness at all mitigated by the dogmatic objectivity with which that group of people least qualified to deal with the realities of life, university professors, preached to a wondering world how civilization had once before been saved by a Germanic people and how it was to be saved again. They then went on to specify precisely what were the earmarks, biologically and psychologically, of the Germanic people. In a manner, of course, this was simply the old dream of a Golden Age refurbished in a smart Prussian uniform.

But it is always dangerous to make dreams specific, and it is doubly dangerous to systematize them. And when this specifically precise and well-ordered dream was fed to a defeated and disheartened people, many of whom had known the Germany

17

of 1900–1910, the most nearly perfect bourgeois paradise the world has possibly ever known, the result was catastrophic. Not only did the old men dream dreams but the young men acted them. Yet since the beginning of civilization this has always held true: the greater the need for a dream, the less care is bestowed in the selection of the stuff of the dream.

CHAPTER II

THE ILLUSION OF THE CONFUSED LATE COMERS: THE NORDIC MYTH

IT is a trite but obvious fact that no one is ever grateful for being taught. So difficult is it for the average man to escape from the apron strings of his parents, and yet so important is it that he break these ties if he wishes to grow up, that more often than not he can only remember the struggle for independence and for individuation. What holds true for an individual holds equally true for a people. Being instructed means that one once needed instruction, and that is frequently an unbearable memory for individuals or nations when they no longer need schoolmasters and are striking out on new paths and on their own initiative.

This feeling of annoyance and humiliation is heightened when the instructor is either inferior or superior to one's self, or when one has not been an apt pupil. Doubtless Crete felt no humiliation at being taught by Egypt nor Greece at being taught by Crete. So in the past generations American scholars felt it no degradation to be under the tutelage of England and Germany, nor Japan in sitting at the feet of Europe. But there are peoples, just as there are individuals, who are not apt pupils and for whom instruction is an arduous and, in their view consequently, a not altogether necessary preliminary for maturity or individualization. They are glad when school is over or when the schoolhouse has been destroyed by flames. Yet manifestly as long as they are living in a world where it is the proper thing to go to school, they must either prove that going to school is an illusion or build imitation schoolhouses of their own or, finally, rebuild the particular schoolhouse that has been destroyed.

Now, whether we like it or not, the only school that existed for Western Europe until approximately the year A.D. 600 was the civilization of the Mediterranean, more specifically the Graeco-Roman. Little is to be gained by insisting that, if a given people had been left alone, it would have developed its own civilization. First of all, they have not been left alone nor have they wished to be left alone, and, second, all the evidence at our disposal indicates that peoples do not mature significantly when left alone. The genus *homo* evolved once. Biologically speaking, there is no reason why it should not have evolved a number of times. It so happens that it did not. Similarly, truly complex civilizations developed exactly twice, conceivably three times—in the area stretching from Egypt to Chinese Turkestan and India, in China, and possibly in Mexico and Peru. In many parts of the rest of the world man had existed just as long as in these areas. In fact, important advances had been made everywhere throughout Europe, Asia, and Africa. Yet nothing had come of them. Apparently civilization, as we conceive it, is not an inherent trait of man, nor has he always achieved it even when the conditions, economic and political, were propitious.

We cannot here pause to speculate why it developed in the Mediterranean and China and nowhere else. Let it suffice us that it did develop there, and that the nations on the periphery had either to come to terms with it or erect strong and adequate barriers against its encroachments. In Europe the people on the periphery were the Celts, the Germans, and the Slavs. The contact of the Slavs with this major civilization was indirect and late and was further complicated by the Tartar invasions from Asia. The Celts, being closest to the Romans, came to grips with it first, proved apt pupils, and were eventually completely overwhelmed. The Germanic tribes, who had probably come originally from South Russia and the upper Danube, found themselves squeezed between the Celts who were on the point of being Romanized and the Slavs with whom they were deadly enemies. That part of their country directly exposed to Roman influence was small but large enough, nevertheless, for Roman influences and Roman legions to make considerable progress. It is not too much to say that the prospects for a Roman conquest of the Germanic tribes were, at first, as bright as those for the Celtic tribes had been a century before. Then unfortunately came the defeat and annihilation of the Roman cohorts under Varus in the pesky Teutoburger forest, where a monument to the German leader Arminius now stands.

Nothing in the whole history of Germany has had such disastrous and wholly evil influences as this unexpected victory. To it are directly traceable most of her ills. For the Germans to glory in that victory shows how confused and muddled they have essentially remained. For what did that victory bring them? It did not alter their fundamentally unstable position between the Celts and the Slavs; it did not give them peace and recognition. On the contrary, it increased the old turmoil and led to neglect and indifference on the part of the Romans and the Romanized Celts. Had they been able subsequently to ward off Roman influence, although it is somewhat doubtful whether they could have held their own against the Slavs, they might, nevertheless, have maintained their own localized civilization as long as the latter. But this is the one thing they could not and would not do. Forces within and without were impelling them to draw

22

ever closer to the Italian peninsula. They insisted upon overwhelming it and became less German with every step southward that they took. For anyone to contend that they added virility to a fast-deteriorating stock or reinvigorated a decaying culture is a sheer misreading of the facts. Indeed it was just the contrary. They lost their virility and gained a partial acquaintance with the Roman civilization at a time when it had ceased to be an activating principle for law and order. They might have been spared this had the mist of the Teutoburger Forest and the incapacity of a Roman general not led to their lamented victory.

But let us put the most generous construction we can upon the Germanic invasion of Italy and regard the Germans there as the free gift of a magnanimous free-born race to a decaying culture. Let us think of them as martyrs in the cause of civilization, gladly giving up their healthy virtues, their typical physiognomy, their Nordic honesty and directness, and their mother tongue. What, however, of their brethren in the glorious pine forests of the north, would not they, at least, retain their pristine virilities for a long time? The Germans of the nineteenth century, particularly after 1871, believed they had. The despised Heine insisted that:

> Deutschland hat ewigen Bestand,
> Es ist ein kerngesundes Land.[1]

[1] Forever Germany will stand,
It is a sound and virile land.

Health, then, the health that comes from an unspoiled constitution and an unimpaired natural vigor, is the trait that, according to German poets and scholars, has always characterized the German and the Nordic mind. This health, they would seem to contend, showed itself when they defeated the Roman legions in A.D. 17, when the great Frankish king Charlemagne resurrected the Roman Empire on that fateful Christmas in A.D. 800; when the Saxon Martin Luther freed Europe from the slavish sense of order and meaningless religious formalism of the Roman Church, the inheritors of the Roman glory; when the Teutonic knights pushed the Slavic tribes out of eastern Germany; and when, finally, a united Germany overwhelmed the descendants of the Romanized Celts in the Franco-Prussian wars. It is exhibited by the Gothic conquest of Spain, by the Gothic and subsequent Lombard conquest of northern Italy, by the Norman conquest of northern France, of England, and of Sicily. Look at the physique of these northern tribes, they exclaim: tall, robust, blue-eyed, and flaxen-haired. Behold their inborn traits: a laughing heart, a will of steel, a child's simplicity, and the *Weltschmerz* that assails a mature man's mind when he contemplates the contrast between his glowing longings and ideals and the world of sordid reality. "All that we have ever wanted," so runs the persistent refrain of their poetic pleadings, "is the right to lead our own lives, in our fairy-infested woods, with the gods of Valhalla at our side. This we have never been permitted to do. At all times we have had to defend ourselves against the foreigners. When they come in force, whether it be the Roman Varus, the Hun Attila, or the Corsican Bonaparte, we have been able to defeat them, but we are helpless against their insinuating wiles. Long ago would we have been lost, completely absorbed and obliterated, had it not been for our eternal health and simplicity. This it is that enables us to throw off centuries of thralldom at one blow and leaves us, as we had always been, untouched and undefiled. And even, when, fallen upon evil times, our own people turned against their true nature, we languish on foreign soil, the eternal Germany floats as a golden mirage before our eyes and we sing:

> Ich hatte einst ein schoenes Vaterland
> Das küsste mich auf Deutsch und sprach auf Deutsch—
> Ich liebe dich!
> Es war ein Traum.[2]

But this is only one aspect of the German genius. Not merely are they presumably the possessors of perennial health and youth, but theirs is the mission to bestow on an ailing mankind new health and new youth. The argument is a familiar one and is based upon the achievements of the Germanic countries since Luther's time as contrasted with those of

[2] Once I possessed a lovely Fatherland
There I was kissed in German, in German told,
"I love you!"
It was a dream.

southern Europe. It is in the northern lands, England, Holland, and Germany, that the great achievements of modern science took place and the modern capitalistic system grew up; it is in Holland and Germany where were laid down the foundations of modern art; in Germany where modern music developed and the final stones were placed on the philosophic edifice begun, it is true, by the Frenchman Descartes, given significant form and content by the Englishmen Locke, Berkeley, and Hume, but a final and permanent context only by the Germans Leibnitz, Kant, and Hegel. It is these same Germanic countries which introduced culture among the backward Slavic tribes of eastern Europe, prevented chaos in Italy, opened up the new world, and Europeanized Asia and Africa.

We are to argue from the known to the unknown, they urge us. Surely never in the history of the world have there been so much comfort, so much health, so much consideration for others as in the nineteenth and twentieth centuries; never have so many people been allowed to participate in their own government, never have their individual rights been so carefully safeguarded, and never before have man's thoughts reached out so far, so profoundly, and so effectively. With the exception of France, no one will deny that this achievement must be ascribed to the Germanic peoples—England, Germany, Holland, and the Scandinavians, and their colonies in the new and old world. In Spain and Spanish

America, in Portugal and the Portuguese colonies, in Italy, Russia, the Balkans, there have, until recently, been unrelieved poverty and religious and political obscurantism. France is the solitary exception and what part of France has participated in this new world? Northern and central France; that part of France which is historically, and even biologically, Germanic in origin. Similarly, northern Italy, where most of the wealth of that country exists, where the people are industrious and live ordered lives, are these men and women not descendants of the Germanic Lombards? Finally, where does the little stamina that exists in Russia come from? From the achievements of the descendants of the Germanic adventurer Rurik and from the German colonists that Peter the Great and his German successor Catherine the Great had settled there. If Czechoslovakia is today so stable and wealthy, to what is this to be ascribed? To its complete Germanification.

Since none of these statements can seriously be denied or, at least, could not have been denied two generations ago, why have we not the right to inquire, first, whether there are not certain traits that have characterized the Germanic peoples since they appeared on the stage of history and, second, why is it not logical to assume that the physical traits they possess are not correlated with their mental ones and their peculiar achievement? It is at this point that difficulties appear and we have our first introduction to the nature of the illusion

27

which has misled those who have built up the doctrine of Nordic or Teutonic superiority.

What does the known history of the Germanic peoples tell us? It is customary to begin such inquiries with Tacitus' description of the Germans in his famous *Germania*. We know, of course, that Tacitus was not the least bit interested in giving an unbiased and scientific account of a people. The Germans, although to him an uncouth tribe of barbarians, were credited with traits that he wished to emphasize in his denunciations of his own times and his own people. But even if we were to accept all his characterizations as true, the picture he draws of the Germans is in no way different from that of hundreds of other primitive tribes in many parts of the world who have a loose-jointed democratic social organization. Dislike of restraint, individualism, a strong religious feeling, martial ardor, hospitality, and conviviality, all these traits are found in societies on a certain economic level, whether their members belong to the White, the Negro, or the Mongolian races. The love of freedom under a chosen leader is in no sense a Germanic trait. Yet these apparently unspoiled people possessed customs and superstitions that, even to a contemporary of Tacitus, would have seemed disgusting and revolting. If, indeed, we wish to form some idea of what the general status of their culture was, we must not go to the historian but to a work like Frazer's *Golden Bough*.

As stated before, all the German ills seem to go back to their victory in the Teutoburger Forest. As we view German history in retrospect, that victory meant that Roman civilization was to reach her piecemeal, that she was never to know when it would come and to what extent it would influence her at a particular time.

Christianity, the heir to the Roman civilization, came to the various Germanic tribes at different periods. The Visigoths and the Ostrogoths received its full force only in consequence of their invasions of Spain and Italy, although they had been nominally converted a few generations before; the other German tribes had to wait till the beginning of the eighth century and then it was relayed to them by a Romanized Briton St. Boniface. Throughout all this period (A.D. 400–700) the various Germanic tribes pushed from place to place, waged a most relentless war upon one another. Not even the most exaggerated accounts of the atrocities attributed to the so-called uncivilized tribes of aboriginal America, Africa, or Oceania can vie with the cruelties perpetrated by the Germans upon one another. Then, before their western branch, the Salic Franks, had been completely saturated with Roman Christian culture, and shortly after those beyond the Elbe had been initiated into it, the genius of one of their leaders, Charlemagne, added to their ultimate confusion by his triumphal invasion of Italy. This led to the complete Romanization of France and to

another premature and disastrous victory for the
peoples of Germany proper—premature because
they had but recently come into intimate contact
with Christianity and could only be rendered more
confused by a Germanic triumph; disastrous because it inevitably led to a false evaluation of their
importance and because it was so short-lived.

What these Germans were like we know from a
number of epic poems they have left us, the famous
Nibelungenlied and *Gudrun*. If the *Nibelungenlied* is a
picture of the German character, we can best sum it
up in one phrase—the glorification of intemperance,
intemperance in hate and in love, in action and in
thought. The element of gentleness and of normal
human sympathy is, in this famous poem, associated
not with the German hero but with the Romanized
Hun Attila (Etzel) and the Romanized Goth
Theodoric the Great (Dietrich von Bern). For
anything comparable with these orgies of blood and
frenzied murder lust, we have to go to the ritualized
cruelty of the Iroquois Indians in the treatment of
their enemies, as described in the *Jesuit Relations in
America*. Nor was this gratification of an undis-
ciplined murder instinct confined merely to the
Germans proper. We find it among the Franks and
among the Scandinavian groups. The *Eddas* are full
of it.

Like all peoples whose ideal is military prestige,
personal courage and tribal loyalty loom large.
So it does among the Ashanti of West Africa, among

Kipling's Fuzzy-Wuzzy, among the Dakota and the Iroquois Indians. *Deutsche Treue und deutscher Muth*, this old German loyalty and courage, with their *furor teutonicus* and the berserker rage, have their counterpart in the Crazy-Dog madness of the Crow Indians and the running amuck of the Malays. In other words, these characteristics are not German; they are not local but simply inevitable aspects of a certain economic order, of certain political and social crises. Where that order exists, they exist; when that order returns, they return. Only this we must add: so little inured has man everywhere become to a rational mode of life and thought that this order has hitherto returned with uncontrollable frequency. To this extent then, and only to this extent, is it permissible to speak of the continuity of certain psychical traits among the Germans: first, they have remained in an economic order that calls them forth longer, and reverted to that order oftener, than any other modern European nation; and, second, the consciousness of this economic instability has expressed itself in their civilization by the prestige attached to what might be called a lyrical and introverted mentality. As far as such a mentality is associated with youth, so far only can it be said that the German mentality has a more youthful physiognomy than the French or Italian or Spanish or English.

The lyrical and introverted mentality, however, awakens a responsive chord in the hearts of most

31

individuals as individuals, for it is, in a way, the last stand of the ego against the enveloping rationalization of civilization, against the gradual enlargement of consciousness. Therein lies its appeal to so many of us, and therein lies its appeal to so many Jews. Sophisticated and weary with the burden of an old integrated tradition upon their backs, contact with this lyricism was like a breath of fresh air. Upon the land which has harbored them now for more than fifteen hundred years, whose language even the Slavic Jews speak—for Yiddish is an old German dialect—and so many of whose ancient customs they have retained when the modern Germans themselves have forgotten them, they have in gratitude, particularly the German Jews, bestowed a love and affection which are otherwise unintelligible. For the last seven hundred years this affection has been spurned and rejected. Who can say why? But is it not possibly due to the fact that, by and large, the German Jews have held fast to the poets' delineation of the inherent German virtues and German customs more fundamentally and more loyally than the Germans themselves? To speak only of minor things: it is among the Slavic Jews—the descendants of German Jews— that the old Germanic relationship terms have persisted (*Muhme, Vetter, Eidam, Schnur*,[3] etc.); that individuals still bear the names typical of the true Germans of the ninth century (Loewe, Hirsch, Baer,

[3] Aunt, uncle, grandfather, daughter-in-law.

Wolf, Hinde[4]) and that mead, the Meth of the Nibelungen heroes, is still drunk.[5] And who is it that has, in these troublous days, kept true faith with the greatest impersonations of German genius —Goethe and Beethoven and Kant? German Jews. I speak of this not with any ulterior motive in mind but as an indication of the fascination that German lyricism and introversion has exercised on a sophisticated and somewhat overrationalized people.

It is then, at best, an idealized version of traits flowing from an unfortunate concatenation of circumstances with which those German poets and professors responsible for the official theory of a Teutonic and Nordic mentality are dealing and not with anything inherent in the German race. It is easy to see why this theory has been perpetuated. Not only did the Germans themselves accept it but it appealed strongly to the sophisticated, over-mannered Italians and French, just as it had to the German Jews. Its highest religious expression was mysticism and its characteristic emotional expression, sentimentalism. Both reached their culmination in the Romantic movement of German literature which began in the third decade of the eighteenth century and swept over the whole of Europe. But we must not anticipate.

The sudden success of the Germanic chieftain Charlemagne was followed by an equally sudden and

[4] Lion, Deer, Bear, Wolf, Hind.
[5] During the Passover week.

long-continued anarchy. But anarchical as the political conditions became, the success of Charlemagne did at last bring Christianity fully to the Germans and overwhelmed them with direct and vital influences from their old neighbors the Romanized Celts, under whose tutelage the Salic Franks had become civilized and had laid the foundations of France. This time, fortunately, no temporary Germanic victory interfered with the free flow of culture from France to Germany, and the result was a partial introduction of gentle manners, of knighthood with its accompanying formalized game of chivalry, and of literature. All this culminated in a notable outburst of intellectual activity and the first great period in German poetry. In the folk epic the *Nibelungenlied*, these influences had already been at work, but here in the productions of the famous Wolfram von Eschenbach and Walther von der Vogelweide—to name only the greatest—they were completely dominant. The Germans of that time possessed a folk poetry of considerable beauty and virility, yet apparently so little inner security did they feel in its excellence and worthiness that it was almost completely swept away at the first touch of foreign forms and foreign manners. Such is the penalty that Germany paid for her victory over the Romans. Everything was new and fascinating and desirable.

The great Wolfram and Walther gave repeated expression to the persistent cry of all deep poets, the contrast between dreams and reality, and this contrast took on a more poignant form for them because they felt keenly how new this culture really was, how transitory it was likely to be, and what dangers threatened it on all sides. They sensed that anarchy and barbarism had been but temporarily trapped. Wolfram takes refuge, like a wise man, in the new peace that a full acceptation of Christianity had brought with it. He recognized the pain of doubt:

> Wo Zweifel nah dem Herzen wohnt,
> Das Wird der Seele schlimm gelohnt.[6]

Walther declares emphatically that, even in his day, coarseness and barbarism were beginning to destroy all the beauty and the art of the Minnesang.[7] The note of sadness that runs through these poets and the particular fascination that religious mysticism had for so many mature German minds in the Middle Ages are a reflection of the feeling of the insecurity of the society of their times and mean fundamentally a flight from reality. They have nothing to do with any inherent German tendencies.

Had the culture to which this great literature bears witness been able to last, many of Germany's subsequent ills might very well have been prevented. But the curse which was upon her, which, initially, had been of her own devising and which, indeed, she has stubbornly insisted upon glorifying ever

---

[6] Where doubt comes near our heart, there the soul receives ill reward.
[7] Unfug, ihr habt gesiegt! (Disorder, you have conquered!)

since, prevented this. That curse consisted in this
fact: that not having felt the fructifying impulse
of Roman civilization for eight hundred years
(A.D. 17–800), the cultural substratum she possessed
was not sufficiently deep or sufficiently well integrated to permit later impulses to take a permanent
hold. Owing, likewise, to the anarchy and turmoil
within Germany during these eight hundred years,
its culture never had an opportunity to crystallize
properly into a unified mass or even to develop any
permanent physiognomy. Not only, then, was it like
clay in the hands of the self-sufficient and well-
organized Church and the formalized literature of
France but it did not even possess enough power to
do more than externally conquer Slavic Prussia.
Caught, consequently, between the breakdown of
their own aboriginal unanchored culture—essentially localized and democratic—the universalism
of the Catholic Church, the impact of the new
France, and the unchristianized Slavs to the east,
the Germans were doubly, triply, confused. Again
they turned to lyricism and produced that amazing
architectural style we call Gothic.

After the literature of the Minnesänger collapsed
about 1250, five hundred years were to elapse before
Germany produced even a third-rate writer. Dis-
orientation had followed upon maladjustment, confusion upon willful anarchy. Gutenberg's invention
of printing and the Italian Renaissance of the
fourteenth and fifteenth centuries produced no

marked upheaval in their life, no raising of their general cultural level, no great men. Then, when toward the end of the fifteenth century a significant artistic development began with such great figures as Dürer and Holbein and hope for a true integration began anew, the old story was repeated. In the person of Martin Luther and in the revolt known as the Protestant Reformation associated with his name, they again pushed back Rome. This time, however, they could not push it back very far and the only result was the splitting up of their own people into two irreconcilable sections and the sinking of their culture to an appalling depth of squalor and misery and demoralization at a time when France, Italy, England, Holland, Spain, and Italy were laying the foundations for the modern world. In their great need they again took refuge in lyricism and introversion and created modern music.

When they finally disentangled themselves from the débris of Luther's temporary victory, there were literally no more worlds to conquer. Spain, France, and England had appropriated the New World. The foundations of modern science, philosophy,[8] and technology had been laid without their help and an economic system had been elaborated to which they were to fall helpless victims.

Then that most amazing of events took place, the great intellectual and artistic awakening which began with the birth of Goethe and ended with the

[8] I am, of course, not forgetting the Germans Kepler and Leibnitz.

advent of the Third Empire in the spring of 1933. It looked, for a time, as if in one supreme effort they wished to make up for all that they had lost; as if finally they were to come into their own and find their rightful place in the sun. The number of their great men was legion and embraced the whole realm of human endeavor, except the fine arts. They attained to a great literature at last, and even though it was small in compass it contained one of the greatest figures in world literature and developed specific forms and qualities which were not only duly recognized by other nations but which influenced foreign thought for the first time in German history. In music they produced something absolutely new. For more than two centuries, one supreme composer was to follow upon another and their music was to sweep everything before it. Only Italy could even remotely threaten their supremacy here. In philosophy and science, although the fundamental concepts and the methodological principles had been established in the seventeenth and eighteenth centuries by Italians, Frenchmen, and Englishmen, they could critically evaluate these achievements and complete the edifice. Even an economic system like capitalism, depending upon specific social developments and technological advances which had been subsidiary in Germany, was incorporated into their own social structure, rationalized, and integrated in a fashion which, for practical effectiveness, was unique. To cap this colossal accomplishment, they perfected a powerful military machine, overwhelmed their hereditary enemy France—taking an almost infantile pride in humiliating her—and achieved a long-postponed unity.

Is it surprising, then, that they were crazed by the contemplation of their greatness and that a wondering world acquiesced in their own assessment?

Yet victory hath its stings and its vanities. A conquering people, when it settles down, is apt to look back upon its past with a certain degree of inquietude. Had it always been so great and, if not, how was this to be explained? Even though it may regard the rest of the world as degenerate and awaiting its quickening touch, the thought that this achievement had come so late is intolerable. An attempt is consequently made to erect a pedigree of greatness. Other nations, civilized and uncivilized, had done this before; still others, unless our order changes radically, will do it in the future. But no nation has possibly ever done it so efficiently as did the Germans of the last quarter of the nineteenth century.

Many circumstances conspired toward this efficiency. Never in the history of the world had there been so well organized a group of chroniclers as the German professors. Never before had a people led so checkered an existence over the centuries. No explanation, no pedigree, consequently, could be satisfactory which contained the slightest contradiction, which was not logically and rigorously consistent and irrefutable. It was a primary requisite that no doubt exist in their own minds. And here it was that their tradition of lyricism and introversion came to their aid.

Essentially the whole force of the German pedigree of greatness is based upon this lyric compensation dream. It was the introversion necessarily associated with this dream that made them feel, with exaggerated poignancy, the tricks fate had played upon them and encouraged their frenzied and infantile urge to cover up their failures, to obliterate the irregularities and implications of the record. For them the old saying did not hold true that nothing is so painful as to remember the days of happiness in times of distress. Indeed it was just the reverse. For them nothing was so painful as to remember, in days of happiness and victory, the times of distress and disgrace. Not only was this attitude of mind an expression of the *parvenu* mentality that seeks justification and status through an ancient coat of arms but it was, at the same time, the continuation of the confused and abject subjectivism that was the outstanding earmark of the German romantic movement of the early nineteenth century.

This lyric longing for an old and good name was, then, clothed in the habiliments of an impeccable scientific inquiry and began with the simple premise that what is common to all is the cause of all. Now what is common to the Germanic peoples? Certain physical traits. Nothing could very well be more concrete. These were a robust constitution, tall stature, light complexion, blond hair, blue eyes, and a long head. But where are Germans to be found who possess all these traits? Not even the most enthusiastic defenders of Nordic and Teutonic superiority claim that all of them can be found frequently united in one individual. Blond hair, blue eyes, and long heads are enough. At a pinch, any combination of these traits or, indeed, one of them alone will suffice. This statement is not meant in jest, as anyone can discover for himself by reading the admirable summary of race theories and criteria by F. H. Hankins.[9]

We must not be amazed at the inability of the promulgators of these theories to notice the inconsistencies, factual and logical, in their argumentation. For they are not—any more than other professors who have attempted to establish pure races or superior racial ingredients, whether they be English, French, Jewish, etc.—in the least concerned with demonstrable evidence. It was the especial curse of the German theorists that so many intangible and indiscernible forces were misleading them. First and foremost was the external apparatus of the nineteenth century scientific method. As we all know, from 1850 to 1900, all of Europe was under the spell of certitude—certitude that things could not change except for the better. It was the scientific

[9] *The Racial Basis of Civilization*, 1926.

method that had largely contributed to this certitude and the scientific method was particularly enshrined in Germany. If by the scientific method a Nordic race could be constructed, then it had certitude. Second, because of the prestige of the learned class, no clear distinction was made between erudition and intelligence, nor did the mass of Germans ever seriously stop to consider whether the sheltered life and the intense specialization of their professors were not a bar to their true and proper understanding of problems that were fundamentally human, and where even the profound application of a scientific method was futile and illusory. That the professors did not grasp this is self-evident. They would not have been professors had they done so. Third, there was the *parvenu* mentality which demanded a convincing and irrefutable demonstration that he had always been as extremely successful, as extremely gifted, and as extremely important as he was now. And over the whole was thrown the traditional German lyricism and subjectivity of which we have spoken so often.

With the typical modern propensity to discuss everything from the viewpoint of so-called metaphysical principles, the German professors—and they were blatantly professors—then proceeded to describe the Germanic genius in terms of the principles of continuity, superiority, and performance.

As just indicated, they had considerable difficulties with the question of the continuity of physical type. Not only did they not agree among themselves, but no one outside Germany would agree with them, and it was rather important, for their whole position, that there should be a certain general consensus of opinion. Nevertheless, by falling back upon the historical fact that Germanic peoples had most certainly overrun large parts of Italy and Spain in the first few centuries of the Christian era, and that they had made permanent settlements there from the fifth century on, a certain degree of verisimilitude was lent to the assumption of a Germanic race with specific and constant physical traits. Since, likewise, only one of the five component elements need be present, it was not difficult to demonstrate the desired continuity and at the same time—this was very important—to postulate that anyone, no matter where he was found, who possessed these traits had Germanic blood. The problem of accounting for dark-haired and round-headed individuals speaking German and contributing to the supposed essence of German achievement, like Martin Luther, for instance, was easily solved by regarding such persons as of alien physical, but of German mental and emotional, type. For, as was to be expected, mental and emotional characteristics were correlated with physical ones. In this manner a perfect mecha-

43

nism was devised, calculated to work in any fashion desired.

The extent to which they pushed their theory of the continuity of physical type and the necessity of having only one of the Germanic criteria is best exemplified by L. Woltmann. Italians like Dante, Michelangelo, and Raphael; Spaniards like Velasquez and Murillo, Frenchmen like Voltaire, Diderot, and Gounod, although having an admixture of the brunet race, "were geniuses not because of, but in spite of, their mixed blood,"[10] an argument that should be quite familiar to Americans because it is their explanation of ability among mulattoes. But more, these Italians, Spaniards, and Frenchmen were all descended from real Germans on their father's side. Giotto, Alighieri (Dante), Bruno, Ghiberti, Vinci, Santi (Raphael), Vecellio (Titian), Tasso, Buonarotti (Michelangelo), Velasquez, Murillo, Vaz, Arouet (Voltaire), Diderot, Gounod were, respectively, Jothe, Aigler, Braun, Wilbert, Wincke, Sandt, Wetzell, Dasse, Bohurodt, Velahise, Moerl, Watz, Arwid, Tietroh, and Gundiwald! Woltmann even forgot that Vinci and Vecellio, for instance, were simply the names of towns. Of such stuff, manifestly, are visions made, but for externally mature men to present them in a flimsy scientific guise, and for equally mature men to accept them, indicates only too clearly that specific emotional factors were at work, that we are dealing

[10] Quoted from Hankins, p. 91.

here with the gratification of a long-postponed wish fulfillment, with the illusion of confused late comers attempting to participate in something that they had always rejected when the opportune moment presented itself, but which they were now prepared to accept. Like egoists, they became children and poor sports, and instead of acknowledging their conversion they turned the spit around and tried to prove that they were actually the creators of what they had so consistently rejected.

If it was difficult to obtain either any general unanimity or general acceptance for the theory of a specific Germanic race, it was comparatively easy to do so for the existence of specific Germanic qualities. The world—more particularly Europe—has for many centuries now been accustomed to describing peoples in terms of national characteristics. These have always differed, depending upon the nation with which one started. The Frenchman has different national traits for a German than he has for an Englishman or Italian, and the German genius looks different when viewed by a Frenchman than when viewed by an Englishman or Spaniard. There seem to be two very simple rules followed in such characterizations: first, the more a nation differs from your own the more ridiculous it is and the more definitely inferior; second, the specific differences are those which innately belong to a nation. According to this interpretation, of course, the specific differences are desirable if they are your

45

specific differences and undesirable and essentially reprehensible if they are the other person's. This attitude goes so far that it embraces such inherently accidental things as the language of one's birth.

Who cannot call to mind the eulogies that have been poured on the excellent and altogether superior qualities possessed by one's mother tongue? In spite of the fact that the particular structure of a language is determined entirely by unconscious and accidental factors, a general feeling prevails that nothing mirrors the soul of a people so accurately as their language. Speaking from the viewpoint of non-Germans, the long ponderous and involved sentences, the change in the position of the verb, the detachable prepositions, the building up of word compounds at discretion, are these not all admirably indicative of the ponderous German character with its slow and solid mentality and its dislike of formalization? To the Germans, on the other hand, they mean depth, profundity, elasticity, and every youthful and imaginative quality of mind and heart. All peoples have this perfectly intelligible love of their own language but the Germans of the nineteenth century, because they were so definitely under the domination of their professors, capitalized this love most efficiently and were more worried about keeping their language pure than others. It was part of their program of purity. Everything must be pure—the physical stock, the physical make-up, the language—and it must be

46

pure in obedience to that desire of all *parvenu* civilizations: that their success and greatness have been achieved unaided.

But to return to the question of German mentality. It was essential for the theorists to show what this was, that it had been continuously expressed, and that it was quite different in its implications from what, to the casual or alien outsider, it appeared to be. All the theorists, in assuming a specific German genius, kept before them particularly the marked contrast between German lyricism and mysticism, on the one hand, and the rigorous and utterly unemotional philosophic system of Kant as well as the equally rigorous and majestic forms of the Bachian music, on the other. This contrast gave them the *Leitmotifs* of the romantic and manifestly adolescent opera they composed. There are two such motifs, *Minne* and *Treue* (love and fidelity), and both have, so to speak, their external and their internal side. Their external aspect is sexual desire and the *furor teutonicus*, their internal aspect, "the quiet yearning thought for the elect of one's heart,"[11] and the courageous all-sufficing and steadfast loyalty and fidelity to kinsmen, friends, and one's promise. Together, *Minne* and *Treue* gave rise to a third trait, which the German theorists regarded as basic, *Innigkeit* (inwardness).

[11] "Das stille sehnende Denken an die Erwählte des Herzens," so the famous Germanist Hermann Kluge defined the true meaning of *Minne*.

This it is that transforms what among other nations would merely be clear, cold, brilliant thinking, into a fundamental, warm, and profound penetration of essences. The abstruse and forbidding terminology introduced into philosophy by the successors of the great philosopher and scientist Leibnitz, and subsequently adopted and rendered even more complicated by Kant and Hegel, had much to do with the success with which the rest of Europe accepted the German evaluation of themselves and this, in turn, naturally reenforced the belief in the correctness of their analysis.

No matter what work on German culture one picks up, if it is written in the nineteenth or twentieth centuries, the themes of German fidelity and inwardness will be developed from the very beginning. In that horror-inspiring blood bath which is the theme of the *Nibelungenlied*, German scholars actually claimed to see the highest poetical expression of German fidelity and loyalty (*das hohe Lied der deutschen Treue*). Professor Kluge even insists that what to us seems the inexpressible lust and weakness of the hero Siegfried is but an expression "of that pure deep love which must end tragically because of its fullness."[12] And it is this same divine love that transforms Siegfried's wife from a simple-minded Gretchen to a bestial and treacherous

[12] *Geschichte der deutschen Nazionalliteratur*, p. 39, 1931. "Das hohe Lied der Minne, der reinen, tiefen Liebe, die tragisch endet, weil ihr Übermass mit Leide lohnet."

48

murderess. In similar fashion did the poet Hoelderlin sing at the end of the eighteenth century:

Sacred heart of my people, my Fatherland
All-suffering, like mother-earth you sit
Silent, reviled, though from your depths
Their very best have they suckled.
From you came the essence of thought, its fruition.
Gladly they plucked your fruit, though they scorned you . . .
O Land of deep serious genius,
Land of love! . . .

Thus poets have always sung whether their names were Hoelderlin or Euripides, Shakespeare, Wordsworth, or Rupert Brooke, and they have sung so enchantingly and convincingly because they have always dealt with a time that never was on land or sea, and with the consecration that comes from dreams. Even the mocker Heine felt this. And do not the people from whom he has sprung still say with the Psalmist,

> If I forget thee, O Jerusalem,
> Let my right hand forget her skill.
> Let my tongue cleave to the roof of my mouth!

But to have taken it seriously, to have thrust it violently into the arena of real life, into the realm where egotism, self-seeking and unkindness are the dominant mainsprings of our actions, and then to have wept, whined, murdered, and dealt death and injustice in every direction, that has been reserved for the Germany of the twentieth century. Unmindful of the advice of the greatest man she ever pro-

49

duced, that they guard themselves against hating life and fleeing to the desert simply because all their springtime dreams did not mature, the Germans became embittered. Instead of hating life, however, and fleeing to the desert, they did something infinitely more stultifying and infinitely more dangerous for themselves: they stayed in the very midst of life and enclosed themselves in a tight-fitting armor of steel—in an adolescent dream, clothed in the verbal panoply of a scientific approach. That their tortuous history needed the sanctuary of dreams no one would possibly deny. Indeed no one will deny that theirs has been a tragic fate and that they are not to be held responsible for that initial victory against the Romans in the Teutoburger Forest. But, surely, they might have recognized by this time that the great periods of their history correspond to the periods in which they have been greatly influenced by foreign thought and culture, that it is then they have come into their own and made unique and significant contributions to culture, and that they fall into senescence and crudity as soon as they retire to their tight-fitting armor. This happens, of course, to all peoples.

It is for this reason, therefore, that it behooves them to recognize the fact that a carefully constructed theory of a German or Nordic race is but the compensation myth of confused late comers, of people whose historical rhythm has not synchronized with that of the rest of the world and who have, in consequence, always come to the table too late and with a poor appetite. It simply is not true for them to insist that they prefer to eat alone. Eating is one of the most inherently social of pastimes. To eat alone may have certain advantages, but the disadvantages are far greater. It almost always leads to disaster for the diners at the table and for those who have already partaken of the meal. That is why the creators of the Third Reich may well contemplate the future with dismay. The effects of the battle in the Teutoburger Forest as well as of the Reformation and the Thirty Years' War are before them.

CHAPTER III

THE TORCH OF CIVILIZATION: FROM THE STONE AGE TO TODAY

ONLY when a simple and undeveloped civilization is influenced by a more mature and complex one does it function significantly. Yet so deeply ingrained is personal vanity in the human race that every individual and every nation wishes to be original, to be the first to have performed a certain task or deed, invented a particular implement or machine, stumbled upon a new thought. The completion of an edifice is always regarded as less remarkable and less indicative of ability and significance than its inception. What thoughtful person has not been appalled and chagrined at the mad scramble of the major civilizations of modern Europe—England, France, Italy, Spain, and Germany—to demonstrate their inherent originality. A Frenchman or German or Italian may, for instance, grant that a given invention was perfected by an Englishman but insist vehemently and patriotically that it was originally invented by a member of his own nationality. Even great men like Newton and Leibnitz engaged in such puerilities. Their infantile jealousies and bad sportsmanship had national repercussions; indeed, even affected the development of thought. To a dispute about priority, more than to any other cause, is the decline of British mathematics after Newton to be attributed. Englishmen insisted upon using the cumbrous method and notation of Newton and patriotically paid the price of having the continental mathematicians outstrip them completely. Apparently it was more important to be English than rational.

If it is priority that matters, however, and if it is true that originality is the primary virtue in all mental operations, then, surely, the crown must be awarded to the peoples of the Old and New Stone Ages who, with nothing more to guide them than an instinctive optimism, laid the foundations upon which all of us have subsequently built. They first devised our basic implements, instituted agriculture, domesticated our plants and animals, invented durable structures, and created the arts of peace and war. Without these fundamentals, civilization would have been impossible. But these discoveries cannot be ascribed to any ancestors of the living races of today except in the most indirect manner. They are the achievements of peoples and races no longer in existence.

In our cultured arrogance we are inclined to look down with amused scorn upon those who seriously contend that real inventive genius was involved in the discovery of the bow and arrow or in the working out of the principles underlying the accuracy and effectiveness of a weapon like the returnable boomerang. Yet until the invention of dynamite by Alfred Nobel, in the late nineteenth century, no fundamental change had taken place in the principles of propelling a missile which were first worked out in the bow and arrow. To our very remote ancestors—the proto-Mongolians, proto-Mediterraneans, proto-Alpines, proto-Nordics—must we ascribe the completion of the edifice begun by these early and extinct races. Their pace was slow, but possibly not so slow, considering the circumstances, as the time required for the Germanic tribes to absorb Graeco-Roman civilization.

Twelve thousand years intervene between the discoveries of pottery and glass, and another two thousand elapsed before porcelain, which is simply pottery completely vitrified, appeared. If it is priority, then, that is the vital consideration, let us raise a monument to the unknown and lowly founders of culture who began their work a hundred thousand years ago and award a second prize to those cousins, five hundred generations removed, who, by the year 8000 B.C., had discovered everything basic to our civilization except the use of metals, the art of writing, and the machine.

The evolution of the ceramic arts from pottery through glass to porcelain brings us face to face with the whole problem of the contributions made to culture by different peoples and different races.

The peoples who first invented pottery were certainly members of the white race, belonging, in fact, to two divisions of it, one long-headed and the other round-headed; the Egyptians who invented glass were a thoroughly mixed white race and the Chinese who invented porcelain are, of course, Mongolians. But when we turn to the very basis of all civilization, the achievements made during the Old Stone Age, beginning one hundred thousand years ago, we cannot make out a good case for any of the ancestors of our present races. The race existing at that time, the Neanderthal, has completely disappeared, and none of the living races— White, Mongolian, and Negro—seems to have been differentiated as yet. If a case can be made for any of them, it is for the Negro. For the white race all we can say, or possibly hope, is that they are, in some degree, descended from the Cro-Magnon race which flourished, in Europe, from the years 25000 to 10000 B.C. The brain of the latter seems to have weighed 15 to 20 per cent more than that of any modern European. The Cro-Magnon peoples were associated with the highest phases of the culture of the Old Stone Age and it would naturally please

Caucasians to have had them as their ancestors, even if that requires the admission that the latter have greatly deteriorated in mind and body from their remote progenitors.

The presence of apparent ancestors of the Negro race in this primary period of human culture would mean that negroes have been in contact with civilization for more than thirty thousand years, a fact that is correlated with the existence of numerous stations of the Old Stone Age civilization along the whole coast of East Africa as far as the Cape.

Assuredly the first epoch in the history of civilization was the most difficult, for it must have been hard for man in those early days, so soon after his differentiation from some apelike progenitor, to have faced himself and, having faced himself, to have had the courage to go on with the assumption that the world was worth being won. Surely he must have fortified himself with dreams and with the optimistic faith that he would change.

In the second epoch, the New Stone Age, appear the ancestors of our present races and subraces, White, Mongolian and Negro. They were already mixed then—mixed, that is, in the sense that each one of these three main divisions contained a certain percentage of individuals having some of the traits of the other.

From the very beginning the white race seems to have been more mixed than the others, for whereas the Negro is overwhelmingly long-headed and the

Mongolian overwhelmingly round-headed the Caucasian is both. To account for this variability, some competent scholars regard the Caucasian race as either constituting a sport variation of the Mongolian race or, better, as having sprung from a mixture of a proto-Mongolian stock and a proto-Caucasian stock. Possibly, after all, Neanderthal man, who was long-headed, did leave some descendants who then mixed with the proto-Mongolians.

Wherever they came from, however, the white race is predominant in the Neolithic culture of both shores of the Mediterranean and Western Europe in general, not only the varieties of today but varieties that no longer exist. The well-known anatomist Elliot Smith predicates, as the founders of the early Neolithic culture of the Western World, a race of long-headed brunets, of small stature, with scanty hair on body and face, relatively broad nose, a feeble jaw, and a skeleton somewhat suggestive of effeminacy in its build. These people, he claims, once occupied the British Isles, France, both sides of the Mediterranean, Egypt, the whole peninsula of Arabia and the shores of the Persian gulf, Sumer, Mesopotamia, Syria, the coastal parts of Asia Minor, Anau in Turkestan, and Indonesia, both the mainland and the archipelago. The features they had in common were a white skin—never, however, of the florid or reddish-white variety of the Nordic race—and a long head. If they can be identified with any modern group, it is the so-called Mediterranean. But at best even that identification is only partial. The race which we call Mediterranean today is, in so far as it has any special physiognomy, probably simply a secondary and more unified offspring of this smaller brown race to which Elliot Smith obviously wishes to credit the whole vast achievement of Neolithic culture and its later additions, the invention of a written script, the first formulation of mathematics, and the creation of objective science. Other scholars like Haddon, however, give the Mediterranean race a far more mixed heredity. They would derive it from peoples existing in the latest periods of the Paleolithic, who have merged with later immigrants.

Neolithic culture can, however, at best only partially be explained in terms of this brown race, for following immediately, and intimately associated with them, came an entirely different people, that is, as far as head form is concerned. They had round heads and their home was Asia Minor. To them and their secondary branch, a round-headed but taller group, we may reasonably ascribe the introduction into Europe before 4000 B.C. of the following cultural elements: cultivated grains and fruits, domestic animals, polished stone implements, painted pottery, weaving and, somewhat later, metal working. To them, too, seem to have been due such fundamental phases of Neolithic culture as the lake dwellings of Switzerland and Italy and the full development of iron technique.

Thus Neolithic culture, like all subsequent complex cultures, is to be credited to a people of the most heterogeneous physical make-up.

Since it seems now definitely proved that the round-headed people reached Europe even in the later periods of the Paleolithic Age, at a time, in fact, when that culture was at its highest, it would be extremely easy, if one were so disposed, to demonstrate that all our culture, the significant early stages and the significant later stages, has been the work of a round-headed variety of man. And if one wished to be exceedingly ungenerous and logical, an excellent case could be constructed to show that the long-heads had always been the disturbers of the peace who destroyed the culture of these round-headed immigrants and subsequently became inoculated with the cultural remnants that they had permitted to survive. But they did not quite know what to do with them and so had to wait for the arrival of more round-heads in order to reunite the badly broken and distorted fragments. For this service the long-heads turned upon them again and this whole *opéra bouffe* began anew.

To a disinterested observer from Mars it might almost have seemed that the long-heads were pessimists and realists, doing their best to discourage the hopeless optimism and romanticism of the round-heads. Doubtless Brutus and Cassius were round-heads who murdered the perfidious long-head Caesar because of his round-headed romantic proclivities, and the round-headed Roman general Varus met his deserved fate at the hands of Hermann in A.D. 17. Yet occasionally the round-heads become quite long-headed in their pessimistic and destructive proclivities. Witness Martin Luther and Adolf Hitler.

To prove that such racial speculation is as justified as much of that which is taken seriously, let me quote the final conclusions of Eugen Fischer, the present rector magnificus of the newly renovated and purified Berlin University:

> There can be no question but that the destiny of peoples and states is definitely and specifically influenced by the racial traits of its carriers. Universal history is simply a segment of racial history [!]. Even if we must deplore the exaggerations and errors of Houston Stuart Chamberlain we cannot possibly escape from the obvious fact that races . . . determine the fate of a people and of a state. . . . The inherited racial criteria . . . are to be thought of as racially determined psychic abilities and potentialities.[1]

The battle between the defenders of the long-heads and the round-heads, begun in the fifties of the nineteenth century, was one of the most unprofitable combats that ever occupied the minds of supposedly serious thinkers. From its very inception it was evident that the data were so deficient, so contradictory, and withal so pliant that almost anything could be proved. Indeed the theorists did prove everything and nothing.

[1] *Rasse und Rassenentstehung beim Menschen*, p. 137, 1927.

This mock-heroic struggle between the long-heads and the round-heads was fought in terms of the Aryans and non-Aryans, the Nordics and the Alpines. But even those scholars who wrote the most glowing panegyrics about the Aryans were rarely even agreed upon the traits with which they wished to endow them. Some, indeed, made them round-headed and considered not the Nordics but the Celts as the original Aryans! The consensus of opinion of the more realistic anthropologists for the last two generations has been fairly definite. No Aryan race ever existed. At best we can speak of a common Aryan language. But, nothing daunted, the Aryan apologists immediately faced about and began a most amazing glorification of the so-called Aryan language. The contribution of the Aryans to the people they had conquered thus became attenuated to a superiority of their language and the mentality it engendered. It was neither their higher material culture nor even their superior physique.[2]

Let us, however, leave this inherently romantic and infantile attempt to correlate ability with race and, bearing in mind that peoples belonging to races now extinct laid the foundations of our culture, pass on to the achievements of the White and

[2] CHILDE, V. GORDON, *The Aryans*, pp. 211–212, 1926. Although a man of real distinction in his chosen field, Childe actually lets his pen write the following perfectly ridiculous sentence, "The Nordic [Aryan] superiority in physique fitted them to be the vehicles of a superior language."

Mongolian races. The Negroes did not participate in the development of the Neolithic culture and those that followed, owing to purely geographical and accidental circumstances. It was passed on to them, however, and they developed cultures of their own, of intrinsic interest and importance, just as did the American Indians, the Polynesians, and other groups. These cultures were, in many ways, the equal of our own—certainly the equal of our own until the Greeks arrived. If a high degree of economic advance and efficiency, a rich artistic development, an amazing prose and poetry, and a complex religious development are the earmarks of a great and advanced civilization, the Negroes of West and East Africa, the Polynesians, and the American Indians of Mexico and Peru possessed it. Surely it is a strange and thoroughly reprehensible artistic obscurantism that would extol the poetry, wisdom, and religiosity of the psalms and not give a high measure of praise to the following hymn of the Yoruba of West Africa:

The sun shines and sends its burning rays down upon us,
The moon rises in its glory.
Rain will come and again the sun will shine.
And over it all passes the eye of God.
Nothing is hidden from him.
Whether you be in your home, whether you be on the water,
Whether you rest in the shade of a tree in the open,
He is there, your master.
Did you think that because you were more powerful than some
    poor orphan,

You could covet his wealth and deceive him,
Saying to yourself, "I cannot be seen?"
So then remember that you are always in the presence of God.
He will some day reward you for your deed.
Not today, not today, not today!
But some day he will give you your just reward,
For thinking in your heart
That you have but cheated a slave, an orphan.
He will some day reward you for your deed.
Not today, not today, not today!

And with all respect for the poems that have been written inciting man to war from the days of the Greek Tyrtaeus to the German Lissauer's *Hymn of Hate*, I know of none as beautiful, as profound, and as likely, unfortunately, to be so efficacious in attaining its purpose as the following one from the Papago Indians of Arizona.[3]

Is my food so much to me
That I should eat what I have and all day sit idle?
Is my drink so much to me
That I should take the sweet water poured out
And all day sit idle?
Is my wife so much to me
That I should gaze upon her
And all day sit idle?
Is my child so much to me
That I should hold it in my arms
And all day sit idle?

It was uncontrollable, my desire.
It was black dizziness.

[3] Collected and translated by Ruth Underhill through whose kindness I here reproduce it.

I ground it to powder and therewith I painted my face.
It was black drunkenness
I tore it in shreds and therewith tied my hair in a war-knot.

Then did I hold firm my well covering shield
And my hard-striking club,
Then did I hold firm my well strung bow
And my smooth, straight flying arrow.
To me did I draw my far-striding sandals
And fast I tied them.

Over the flat land then I went striding
Over the embedded stones I went stumbling
Under the trees in the ditches I went stooping
Through the trees on the high ground I went hurtling
Through the mountain arroyos I went brushing quickly.

But let us return to the Mediterranean, to
Europe, and to Asia. After the economic and
cultural foundations had been laid in the Neolithic
Age proper, great civilizations sprang up, about the
years 5000–4000 B.C., if not earlier, in Northern
Africa, Asia Minor, and northern India. Apart
from great material advances made, they added one
element to our cultural inventory which has
revolutionized the world: writing.

In no discovery, unless it be the sciences of Europe
since the sixteenth century, have so many people
participated. The first stage of writing, the syllabic,
was arrived at, possibly independently, by a number
of races of heterogeneous physical type: the Egyptians who belonged to a mixed race, among whom
predominated the physical characteristics of the

modern Mediterranean race; *i.e.*, they were overwhelmingly long-headed; the Hittites of Asia Minor, a round-headed people; the Sumerians of Asia Minor, long-headed and round-headed in almost equal intermixture; and the peoples of Mohenjo-Daro, of the Indus Valley, who were probably Dravidian in origin, *i.e.*, belonged to the original population of India, a people with whom the native Australians have frequently been brought into relation. Independently, and much later, the Chinese and the Mayas of Mexico and Central America devised an effective syllabic alphabet. And while China was devising its alphabets, Semitic tribes clearly of mixed physical type developed the phonetic writing upon which all alphabets have since been based.

The languages spoken by the inventors and perfectors of the alphabet were even more diverse than their physical type. Egyptian and Semitic unquestionably belonged together; Hittite belonged to the Indo-European group; the relationship of Sumerian is doubtful but it is possibly a member of the Turkish linguistic family; the language of Mohenjo-Daro was probably Dravidian; Chinese is a unit by itself; and the Maya of Mexico is unquestionably a mixture of certain aboriginal dialects of America.

What writing has meant to the human race need not be stressed. It is self-evident. Only in this way could the past be remembered with any degree of accuracy and only in this manner could mankind rid itself of too intense an absorption in the past. If not a new type of mentality, it meant, at least, an enlargement of our former mentality and the beginning of our escape from the thralldom of the unconscious. In this tremendous achievement few representatives of the races specifically known today as the Mediterranean, the Alpine, and the Nordic participated. It was the work of mixed, mongrel peoples who probably had proto-Mediterranean, proto-Alpine, and proto-Nordic blood in their veins, not to mention the blood of races about whom we know nothing.

And what of the Nordic race, what were they doing at the time, the race around which the newly adopted German legal code revolves, that code where the conscience of the racially pure Teuton tells him what is right and what is wrong? Possibly they were just then emerging as a special entity. If they started out as a pure race, a somewhat doubtful hypothesis, that purity was soon lost. Yet, pure or impure, what were they doing? At best, decapitating thistles on the shores of the Baltic Sea.

After the invention of writing, no revolutionary change took place in European culture until the Greeks appeared on the scene in their full glory, about 600 B.C. This does not imply that in the great civilizations in Egypt, Crete, Asia Minor, northern India, and China nothing had been achieved

66

between the years 5000 and 600 B.C. Indeed the Greek civilization stands squarely upon the foundations laid down in Egypt, Crete, and Asia Minor. Yet notwithstanding this fact, Western European civilization is based on that of the Greeks in almost every significant respect, even if one of its important phases, Christianity, is the product of Greek and Semitic influences.

The Greeks introduced into the world the spirit of objectivity, the first effective analysis of consciousness, and the first clear-cut statement of the contrast between the mind, on the one hand, and the body and the external world, on the other. Their advent meant a further extension of the domain of the conscious. This, and not their literature or art, gives them their unique place in universal history. Other peoples before them, civilized and uncivilized, have had great literatures and great arts. Today we know definitely that even comparatively simple tribes, without writing and without adequate tools, can achieve true and profound literatures and arts. Our vistas have grown larger, our arrogance and narrow-mindedness smaller. But literature and art spring from an aspect of human nature which is essentially opposed to the development of true objectivity. By themselves they never have led and never will lead to it. None of the civilizations that were so much older than that of Greece succeeded in making those discriminations between the mind and the external world that were necessary and essential for a true understanding of objective reality. And therein resides the greatness of the ancient Greeks.

After all, Plato and Aristotle did, for the first time, state the two fundamental positions that can be taken in any analysis of the relation of the mind and the body, or of the nature of the external world; and they stated it so completely that, on the whole, no thinkers until the seventeenth century improved upon them. And even then, philosophically speaking, they simply gave up an Aristotelian heritage in order to return to the tradition, if not the precise formulation, of Plato. In like fashion it was the Greeks, from the sixth century B.C. onward, who began that conscious and quantitative analysis of the external world which remained truncated because of the victory of the Roman bourgeois civilization and the compromising religious synthesis of declining Greek and Semitic cultures. It was this truncated science that was revivified, reorganized, and completed by the science of modern Europe.

Who were these Greeks? In very early times Greece seems to have been inhabited by the eastern division of the Mediterranean race; *i.e.*, they were long-headed and dark-haired. Throughout the Neolithic it was inhabited by a round-headed race. In the Bronze Age the Cretans, who were a composite of varieties of the Mediterranean peoples with an important addition of round heads swept

68

over the land. Then the Achaeans, a blend of people without much culture who belonged to a proto-Nordic stock with a mixture of round heads, overran the land and they were followed by equally crude and rude round-headed peoples whom we call the Dorians. And it is this unbelievable *mixtum compositum* that, under the influence of Egypt, Crete, and Asia Minor, and after they had adopted a final revision of the alphabet made by a Semitic tribe, gave rise to Greek culture.

The next great revolution in human thought came two thousand years later, with the invention of true machines, the development of mechanical appliances, and the creation of a new scientific method and exact experimental disciplines, whose import it is even now impossible to foretell. Nothing just like it had ever happened before, and in retrospect its truest explanation is to be sought in the hypothesis that the human brain, which, anatomically speaking, is so young, had at last begun to function maturely.

But what people participated in this astounding revolution? Do they belong to a single general physical type, to a circumscribed area, to a specific nationality? And do they speak the same tongue? The facts are before us and not a few have been unearthed by German scholars.

The preliminaries of the scientific renaissance that took definite form in Italy at the end of the fifteenth century are unquestionably to be sought among the Arabs and the Jews. It was they who kept alive the Greek tradition, particularly in medicine; it was they who continued the Greek tradition of mathematics and gave it an entirely new perspective by introducing the Arabic notation and algebra—the two weapons that have made modern mathematics possible and which had come to them from India. To these two we must add the concept of zero which had also come from India. The combination of the three made the work of the Pole Copernicus, the Italian Galileo, the German Kepler, the Englishman Newton, and the Frenchman Descartes possible.

Other factors, too, were instrumental in preparing the condition on which these great men could work and be effective—modern trade and the capitalistic system, the invention of the compass, of movable type, and of rag paper and books. The compass, movable type, and rag paper represent the contributions of China to the western world, and if we add gunpowder our debt to that great civilization is incalculable.

In all these achievements, two distinct races were involved: the Caucasian and the Mongolian. Among the Mongolians we find a mixture even greater than that for the Caucasians. For the Caucasians we have every single variety of that race represented—Mediterranean, Alpine, Nordic—all of them in the most inextricable mixtures and combinations. If we try to associate the achievements of this epoch with specific peoples, we find the following contributions: Trade and the capitalistic system were predominantly the contribution of the Jews, Italians, English, and Spaniards; mathematics that of the Italians, French, English, north Germans, and Jews; physics, until the nineteenth century, that of the Italians, English, French, and Dutch; in the nineteenth century, these same peoples, with the addition of the Germans and the Jews. Chemistry was the creation of the English and the French, although it was in the Germany of the nineteenth century that it celebrated some of its greatest triumphs. Modern biology began in Italy in the early eighteenth century and made definite advances in Germany, Holland, and England at the same period. Essentially, however, its greatness rests upon the achievements of the French, English, Germans, and, within recent times, Americans.

Here we have long-heads and round-heads, blonde and brunet, blue-eyed and black-eyed, short and tall, rubbing shoulders in a most unaristocratic manner, and not concerned in the least about the purity of their blood.

It is thus clear that no physical type was correlated with this revolution, that it took place in a circumscribed area only if we regard Europe as a whole, with the possible exception of Spain and the Balkans, as such. Russia must be included because it was there that some of the most distinctive achievements in the chemistry, zoology, and

71

mathematics of the nineteenth century were made.

In other words, we are in the presence of a fairly well-crystallized European culture, a new entity if you will, but one based on a Greek, Arabic, Jewish, Chinese, and even American Indian heritage, for its two primary foodstuffs are potatoes and maize and its fundamental form of pleasure is a mild narcotic that has surely done more to make man more acceptable to himself than any measure known to him for the last five thousand years: tobacco.

And so was the torch of civilization handed down from one generation to another, in many and diverse ways and by many and diverse peoples, all of them criminally oblivious of the racial qualifications they were supposed to possess or of the unpardonable manner in which their carelessness as to the purity of their blood was to effect the German theorists of the nineteenth century.

CHAPTER IV

THE EUROPEAN ACHIEVEMENT SINCE THE SIXTEENTH CENTURY: THE NEW INSTRUMENT AND THE NEW NATIONALISM

IT has become old-fashioned to insist upon the new deliverance which began for Europe in the fifteenth century and gathered full momentum in the sixteenth. The professional historian of the nineteenth century with his somewhat choked mental outlook, contrasting so strongly with the breadth of his erudition and the intensity of his application to the study of so-called sources, was hardly the person to give us a proper perspective. It was either too large or too small, too enthusiastic or too coldly critical. The twentieth century scholars, consequently, lost interest and faith not only in these older judgments; they lost interest in the very periods themselves. Humanism and renaissance became for them the first indications of the break-up of a unified European civilization—simply preludes to the birth of nationalism.

However intelligible such a view may be as a reaction against the subjective evaluations of the nineteenth century, it is more than unfortunate, for it contributed directly to the perpetuation of a wrong emphasis and an unjustified localization of culture where no such localization had actually occurred. We are all quite willing to admit that there was a European civilization in the twelfth, thirteenth, and fourteenth centuries, with local varieties in Italy, Spain, France, England, Germany, etc. But with the birth of the great national units of the sixteenth century and the breaking up of Christianity into two antagonistic camps, we are prone to speak not of European civilization but of the specific cultures of Europe. That these nations, for various reasons, deluded themselves into thinking so is unquestionably true. Yet even a cursory reading of the facts should make it clear that these claims are based upon purely political considerations and in no way justified the conclusion that the physiognomy of the different countries of Europe had changed so radically and completely that one could speak of a European civilization only when contrasting it with a Chinese or a Hindu.

The difference between the Middle Ages and Europe after the sixteenth century lies in the fact that the universalism or cosmopolitanism implied in the general acceptance of Catholicism was gone. That is all. But another universalism or cosmopolitanism was slowly to take its place, of greater import than the Catholic, for it implied that at last Europe had absorbed those fragments of the Graeco-Roman civilization which had survived the raids of the Germanic tribes and the heavy, if humanly explicable, shroud which early Christianity had thrown around it. The individual cultures themselves, far from having become more differentiated during the last five hundred years, have become a thousandfold less so.

How then, it might be asked in passing, did this interest in establishing national physiognomies and the mad and arrogant assertions that such and such a science, for instance, was an English or a French or a German one develop, if they do not reflect an actual condition? The answer is comparatively simple. What has changed is not the condition but the scholar and the scientist, and they have changed only since the beginning of the nineteenth century, in response to the competition resulting from the large number of people engaged in a given subject, the very factor that has been so important in the tremendous advances taking place during that period. With a freedom to work such as had never before existed in the world's history, there also came an unprecedented development of egotism, such as had perhaps never before existed, expressing itself

75

in the use of the name of respective countries as a glorified adjective and in the exalting of the contributions made by particular scientists and scholars of their own lands. In all fairness, however, it must be said that this distorted individualism first made its mass appearance after the Franco-Prussian war, that, in France, it was a compensation for their defeat and, in Germany, part of the program for establishing an ancient and continuous pedigree. Essentially we are in the presence of a professors' quarrel. How acrimonious, petty, and short-sighted that can be is well-known.

The humanism, the revival of learning in the fifteenth century, was thus a first definite indication that Graeco-Roman civilization had triumphed, that continuity had been restored; and in continuity universalism is always implied. The first effect of this triumph was a critique of the mediaeval state-church. It had served its primary function, that of assuaging Western Europe in an emotional crisis of catastrophic proportions and salvaging Graeco-Roman civilization. Great as had been its services in the course of internationalism and continuity, its internationalism was too narrow, when the full flood of the internationalism inherent in the Graeco-Roman culture again asserted itself, and too specialized to successfully withstand the political and crude nationalism which began in the sixteenth century. Political nationalism is inherently anarchical in itself, but that of Europe since the sixteenth century became doubly so because it not only was in direct opposition to all the forces that now asserted themselves—the Graeco-Roman past, trade and capitalism and modern technology and science—but falsely imagined that a localized political unity was worth striving for and attainable. The mechanism it devised was a return to an absolutism of a far more onerous variety than that of the Church had ever been. Its basis was trade and commerce and its personal reward, comfort, affluence, and power. But because this was so, it carried within its own body the germs that were to destroy it and give rise to the modern mind and the modern temper.

Thus affirmation was followed by negation and ended in a new synthesis, after a fashion that should have delighted the great Hegel. Yet he understood so little of the true implications of his own theory that he actually thought that the absolutist state of William III of Prussia was this new synthesis! This itself is the most complete demonstration of the anarchical tendencies inherent in the new political nationalism, when the preacher of the ideal and the absolute could, within the realm of the practical, come to such abysmal grief.

The mediaeval temper had been unity in variety; the modern temper was to be variety in unity; and this reversal was to take place because the mind, instead of the heart and emotions, was to become the center of interest. The art of emotions Catholicism

77

had plumbed to its very depths, but the art of thinking it had neglected. Whatever thinking had been done had been done in the service of postulates of the heart. Because they were postulates of the heart, however, a quantitative conception of the universe had been impossible; and because they were postulates of the emotions, the concept of a controlled unfolding had been discouraged, if not damned.

It was to the art of thinking the Renaissance recalled man. That meant a return to the Graeco-Roman civilization. The fifteenth and sixteenth centuries with the uncritical enthusiasms of semi-sophisticated people in the presence of a culture in which form ruled supreme at first saw only the ancient art and literature. Yet they needed no masters there. They were too new to real culture, however, to know how to discriminate and so they imitated the older literature and art to the serious detriment of their own. Slowly, however, the threads with Greek science and philosophy were found and the mind came to its own again.

How complete the severance from Greek science had been during the Middle Ages is indicated by the fact that Galileo and his contemporaries began where the Greeks had stopped. How akin thinking not under the tutelage of feeling is, the world over, was proved by the ease with which the scientists from the sixteenth century on completed what the Greeks had begun and immediately passed far beyond them. Only against that particular form of Greek astronomy which the Church had incorporated into its ideology was there complaint.

The explanation for this amazing increment of growth is to be sought not so much in the new instruments like the telescope, thermometer, microscope, as in the fact that the modern mind was functioning again as the Greek mind had done, with the same willingness to take new ideas wherever they were found, with the same interest in objective reality, and with the same absorption in the subject studied, and not in themselves.

Out of all this came the machine, modern mathematics and philosophy, and the modern insistence upon quantitative analysis. And just as had held true in the case of Alexander the Great and the Hellenistic period following, which had taken place over a large area among an inextricably mixed population, so, likewise, did it hold true for this new scientific outburst. It embraced all of Europe with the exception of Spain, Russia, and the Balkans. To speak here of national accomplishments and achievements would be the height of the ridiculous. Not only were these scientists unaware of there being an English or a German or an Italian science but they were fully cognizant of their debt to ancient Greece and to the Arabs—to the Orient in general. It is, again, only in Germany from which a little braggadoccio comes. Jacob Wimpheling in 1507 wrote in language almost recalling that of modern

German professors, "Of no art can we Germans be more proud than of the art of printing which made us the intellectual bearers of the doctrines of Christianity, of all divine and earthly sciences, and thus benefactors of the whole race!" Today we know that printing, *i.e.*, movable type, was not invented by a German or, for that matter, by a European, but that it had been known for more than a thousand years in China before it was "rediscovered" in Europe.

How widely scattered were even the birthplaces of the scientists—and their birthplaces, of course, had nothing to do with their race, culture, nationality, or place of activity—the history of the new astronomy indicates. The earliest figure was the famous Bishop Nicholas of Cusa born in Trier in 1401, a city which had been thoroughly Romanized in the first century A.D. The bishop himself was not even so much of a German as Houston Stuart Chamberlain was an Englishman. He stimulated a young German Peurbach to study astronomy and Peurbach, in turn, became the master of one of the most distinguished scientific men of his time, Regiomontanus. Regiomontanus's birthplace was the distant Koenigsberg in east Prussia, a region that had been wrested from the Slavs two hundred years before and in which Slavic blood predominated overwhelmingly then as it does now. Succeeding him came the founder of modern astronomy Nicholas Copernicus, a Romanized Pole born in the city of Thorn on the Vistula, who received most of his training at Italian universities and who entered the Church. Copernicus died in 1543, and in 1546 the next great mind to occupy itself with the subject was born, Tycho Brahe, a Dane of noble blood who spent a large part of his time in southern Germany. There Kepler, a Protestant born ine xtreme poverty in Würtemberg, came under his influence. Contemporary with him was the great Italian Galileo.

Thus the fundamental principles of the new astronomy were laid down by persons born in places as widely separated as Trier on the Moselle and Thorn on the Vistula, Pisa in central Italy and a small town in northern Denmark; Catholics and Protestants, peasants and noblemen, individuals with long-heads and round-heads, whose native tongues were German, Polish, Danish, and Italian. The whole new structure of astronomy and physics could, however, not be completed before the epoch-making advances of the Frenchman Descartes and the Dutchman Huygens had been made. All these advances were then summarized, reinforced and revolutionized by new experiments and mathematical formulas, and generalized by the Englishman Sir Isaac Newton.

Those who are interested in the question of the respective glory attached to beginning a line of research and its completion are in an embarrassing dilemma here. Assuredly the crown should be equally divided between the ancient Greeks and the

Hindus and Arabs, on the one hand, and a Pole, on the other. Yet not the Arabs, Hindus, or Poles subsequently produced any great astronomers, physicists, or mathematicians. The Germans with Regiomontanus and Kepler in the fifteenth and sixteenth centuries rested on their laurels till the nineteenth; the French beginning with Descartes in the seventeenth have consistently produced great physicists and mathematicians since then; the English, however, fell off woefully after Newton for a century; and the Italians produced no great physicist from Galileo's time to the end of the eighteenth century.

In order to interpret this record in the interests of nationalism, the various nations, in the persons of their professors, have resorted to different types of explanation. The Slavs, beginning with Copernicus, have stressed what they claimed was the freedom from formalistic thought, which made for originality. "What difference does it make," so they seem to contend, "that no Slav accomplished anything between the fifteenth and nineteenth century? We had other things to do. But when great Slavs again turned to mathematics and the experimental sciences, they produced Lobatchewsky who revolutionized the basic principles of the accepted mathematics, and thereby became a precursor of Einstein, and Mendeleef who revolutionized chemistry."

The Germans make much the same claim except that, on the record, they feel they can go further.

"Was not Kepler," they assert, "the mind that made Galileo and Newton possible? And did he not appear at the same time as Luther, who freed Europe from thralldom to an outworn creed? Therein is proof of our originality and courage. This originality is further demonstrated by the appearance of the great Leibnitz in the seventeenth century, who introduced a new weapon into mathematics. Within a few generations came Kant and Hegel, who revolutionized philosophy and completed the structure begun by Kepler. We always begin and we always complete. Even in the discovery of the two Americas, in which we could not participate physically, we participated intellectually and, as usual, we were first. Without the genius of Regiomontanus, whose real name was Johann Mueller, Columbus and Cabot and the whole cohort of navigators, Italian, Spanish, English, French, could never have made their discoveries. And it was we who first gave the New World its name, America—erroneously, it is true."

The French, on the other hand, insist that only in continuity lies greatness. "We may have begun later than the Germans as far as science is concerned, but in some phase of culture we have been supreme since Charlemagne. We were the creators of a new literature which swept over Europe from the twelfth to sixteenth centuries and, in the seventeenth, we continued that tradition, spread the French culture and literature over Europe, and produced the man to whom all the new progress is due, in philosophy, mathematics, and science, Descartes. Since then we have never stopped. On the contrary, we added the greatest art Europe has seen since the Renaissance, and to prove both our continuity and our originality, as well as the varied nature of our accomplishments, we have given the world, since the end of the eighteenth century, the man who created modern chemistry, the man who created celestial mechanics, and, within recent times, the man who introduced the music of the future, not to mention, of course, the French Revolution and the tradition of nationalism and freedom."

The English, with that calmness which comes from an assured and deserved position in the world, spend little time in proving their excellence. But to those who are interested in such games, they say, "We produce great men when and howsoever we please. We are not interested in the principles of originality and continuity. When we choose to have a continuous tradition, we do so. Witness our parliamentarianism and, above all, our literature. When we choose to be original and the first on the scene, we are. Witness Roger Bacon in the thirteenth century and Francis Bacon in the sixteenth and the whole galaxy of scientists who, in large measure, created modern science. When we wish to generalize and complete, we are just as competent. Witness Sir Isaac Newton and Charles Darwin."

84

The Italians say very little indeed. Why should they? They have perfect manners, are fully grown up and have the past of Etruria, of the Roman Empire, of the Florence of the thirteenth to sixteenth centuries—Virgil and Roman law, Dante and Leonardo, Michelangelo and Galileo—to conjure with. If they are reproached with the comparative meagerness of their output in the eighteenth and nineteenth centuries, they can still retort, "What will you? Volta, Galvani, and Marconi, Leopardi and Carducci and the Italian opera, is this not something? Granted that it is not on a par with our earlier achievements. But there is still the twentieth century!" And the chances are overwhelmingly that they are right.

In such puerile manner did men treat one of the greatest advances the human mind has ever made. Manifestly here one individual builds upon another, and there is neither specific beginning nor specific end. If glory must go to some particular person for the invention, let us say, of the telescope, it cannot go to Galileo or any famous scientist but to the children of a Dutch spectacle maker who, while at play, happened by chance to bring together two lenses so that a distant spire became magnified. And the glory of inventing the compass must be given to Chinese toy makers.

To explain the need which the nations of Europe seem to have felt for appraising their accomplishments in this adolescent fashion, we must remember the economic order that was slowly emerging. This economic order was a European achievement in which the Italians, Spaniards, English, Dutch, French, and Jews actively participated. It depended upon trade and commerce and contained within itself a fatal contradiction, for, while its primary aim was in each case to enrich a particular nation, this could take place only by an interchange of goods with another one. Each country consequently attempted to keep its competitor in proper and necessary subjection to itself. The competition, jealousy, envy, trickery that are inevitable in trade and business became transferred to every phase of life, since it was a necessary corollary that a people who were distinguished in material wealth must, of course, be distinguished in every other way. There was sufficient external and visible truth in this attitude for it to appear as incontrovertible. Material wealth does lead to the urge for increasing such wealth tenfold, and from the seventeenth century on this manifested itself in a stupendous technological advance that had been made possible by scientific researches. The attendant comfort and leisure, in turn, meant an opportunity for that inherent artistic ability of all types, which lies dormant in every people, to express itself.

While leisure and security are, however, prime conditions for its appearance, apparently it has a rhythm all its own. The nations among which an unusually great literature developed, for instance, were England, France, Germany, Spain, and Russia, and the greatness of these literatures seems to be in inverse proportion to the degree with which the modern economic structure and capitalism had fastened itself upon them, a fortunate circumstance, indeed, for in the obsessive nationalistic mania that attacked Europe, after the seventies of the last century, those peoples who had made little material progress could point to their spiritual and artistic achievements. This held particularly for the defensive nationalism that developed in Spain and Spanish America.

This economic and technological progress, with its consequent complete triumph of the merchant and trader, transferred their slogans and type of advertisement to every phase of culture—science, literature, art, and music. These became goods which were to be auctioned off and extolled and exaggerated as is proper on such occasions. The argument ran somewhat as follows: Just as, let us say, England manufactured the best steel, so it manufactured the best biology and poetry and, since it was inherent in the Englishman to be a great tradesman, so it was inherent in him to produce great scientists and poets. Since the French economic situation was different, the argument varied. The rationality that made a Frenchman wish to retire and live on his income after he was forty was an expression of the instinctive sense of poise and proportion so characteristic of *la douce*

France. Witness its feeling for form, its hatred of exaggeration, the continuity of its culture. In short, we have a typical bourgeois of Lyon and Lille manufacturing the conditions for his security and French *clarté*, French science, and French art. And so on, *ad nauseam.*

It was left to the Germans, who came last in their economic development, to systematize the tradesmen's slogans and invest them in a pretentious philosophical jargon, a task that fitted in admirably with their latent sense of inferiority. They were abetted in this by the professors, who confused an objective method with the objective arrangement of subjective evaluations, and who thus, with their clandestine rhetoric, became worse than the merchants themselves, for the latter knew they were hawking their wares but the good professors thought they were plumbing the deepest reaches of the national verities.

The high evaluation placed on material progress and the comforts arising through it thus completely obscured the true significance of the forward thrust the human mind had experienced from the sixteenth century on and emphasized transient and specific localizations of ability to the detriment of the whole achievement. As we have said, it was a tradesmen's assessment and a tradesman naturally saw only the political boundaries of his own country. Yet country was an elastic concept, for, while the old core might always remain the same, the limits to which its sovereignty could expand were infinite, determined only by the size of the earth and the successful resistance offered by neighbors.

Such expansions had, of course, taken place before—innumerable times. In such fashion was Alexander's empire built up and Roman hegemony established. But the situation had altered completely. These early conquests had not been tradesmen's conquests and they had been over either simple tribes or decaying cultures. Nor did a group of intellectuals exist who were so thoroughly saturated with the business slogans and technique that they could not think of any other explanation for the success attendant upon the ruthless employment of power except that of inherent national greatness and virility. Since, however, these modern conquests were tradesmen's conquests, the latter imposed not only their merchandise proper but their intellectual merchandise as well upon the conquered. It is not strange, consequently, that the origin of the slogans was forgotten and the evaluations were regarded as inhering in the science, literature, art, music, language, etc., of a nation and subsequently became transferred to the physical traits of the people themselves and the land in which they lived. And so the poets and nostalgic intellectuals spoke with tears in their eyes of *la douce France*, *mein liebes Vaterland*, *England, my England*, and *L'Italia irredenta*. One does not hear peasants waxing eloquent in this way about the soil upon which they and their forefathers have toiled for untold generations. But the poets and intellectuals who have never turned a clod of earth weep bitter tears about the possibility of its desecration by an enemy's foot. They had forgotten that *la douce France* was but another name for vineyards of Champagne, *mein liebes Vaterland* for the potash of Alsace, and *England, my England* for the coal mines of Newcastle. That men should be willing to die for this confusion is their own tragedy; that they should dare to write

> If I should die, think only this of me:
> That there's some corner of a foreign field
> That is forever England. . . .

that is meet cause for tears. For all those young men, who, like Rupert Brooke, died to keep England's markets safe, it is not enough to say in excuse that they were magnificently unprepared for the long pettiness of life. By dying in that cause they did death a disservice, and by extending England's limits thus unduly they gave a false ennoblement to racial arrogance and became renegades to the new instrument forged by Kepler and Galileo and Newton. They thus helped in that malignant subdivision of a glory that was Europe's, that could only be understood when viewed from this larger point of vantage, and substituted a huckster's street cry for a true poet's intuition. They but aided the politicians and professors to create their

90

figures of earth with the lineaments of a glorified John Bull, Marianne, Germania, and Uncle Sam.

It is dangerous enough to invest a living individual with such phantom excellence but to surround a robot with such an aureole is catastrophic, for, in our highly mechanized existence, robots feel they are entitled to the goods of life. They behave like human beings and give themselves a pedigree partly divine and partly human. Is not that the pedigree nationalism and its attendant sycophants racial purity and racial superiority have adopted for themselves? And, since they are robots, what can be done about it? Human arguments have no pertinence, and facts and data which appear as rational and incontrovertible to the human mind have no validity. Validity, truth, justice can only be discussed through the intuitions of a divinely inspired automoton. So we have Dr. Helmuth Nicolai of Germany informing the world that:

Race stamps this code [the new German code]. Our whole new legal system is constructed on the cornerstone of race. There are two kinds of justice—the Nordic or Teutonic kind is something one feels.

The conscience of the racially pure Teuton tells him what is right and what is wrong. The Oriental has no conscience being of a mixed race. He does not perceive what is right as clearly as does the German. That is why the Oriental is obliged to learn law, to read and to write it. We are again binding Germany to the age-old heritage of racialism.

And this Teutonic clarity of vision, of what does it consist? The greatest novelist Germany has ever produced, Thomas Mann, lives in banishment; the German universities have been disrupted, and the man who revolutionized our conception of the world, Albert Einstein, is no longer head of the Kaiser Wilhelm Institute.

And what of the Nordic or Teutonic purity of race? In 1902, among the assuredly purest representatives of this race, in Scandinavia, of 45,000 recruits, 10.7 per cent possessed all its basic traits.

Opposed to this Teutonic clarity of vision, the great Chinese sage, he of necessarily mixed stock, he who fortunately had to learn the law, to read it and to write it, said in his blurred manner:

"When the mind is not present, we look and we do not see; we hear and we do not understand; we eat and we do not know the taste of what we eat."

But to conclude. The tradesman's legitimate method of enhancing the value of his wares became illegitimately and surreptitiously identified with the country in which they were manufactured, with the physical type of the producers, and the achievements of the culture—scientifically, artistically and spiritually—to which they belonged. But such advertisements have fatal defects and actually contain within themselves the seeds of their own dissolution. The high degree of excellence in workmanship and output cannot always be maintained and, because of the very extensive and effective publicity given them, the same world which was apprised of their merits is also likely to become aware of their demerits. Here we have thesis and antithesis again. Under so powerful a catalyzer as the new science and the art of thought which it engendered, a new synthesis was to arise, a pan-Europeanism, a thin cover for the essential internationalism underneath, which alone can hope to cope with racial robots.

CHAPTER V

THE PAN-EUROPEAN ACHIEVEMENT IN THE NINETEENTH CENTURY: THE NEW ART OF THOUGHT

NATIONALISM and racialism, it has become clear, were by-products of an economic order, given shape and respectability by romantic intellectuals and poets, because they could weave them unconsciously into the texture of their phantasy and compensation dreams, and used realistically and cynically by politicians and merchants. The latter were not in the least deluded as to the mythical nature of these robots. With that question, however, they were little concerned. All they knew was that the thesis of racial superiority was an admirable weapon when they were victorious, and the thesis of racial impurity an excellent excuse when they were defeated. Truth was the very last thing for which they strove. Universities with well-stocked libraries and a huge corps of instructors were especially provided to deal with this essentially theoretical and frequently inexpedient subject.

Still, let us linger for a brief moment at her side and shut out, with academic insolence, the sounds of the market place and the pandemonium of the exchange and proceed as though our intellectual and ethical inquisitiveness had conquered our practical fears.

Now if we catalogue the achievements of the various nations of modern Europe in terms of centuries, we arrive at the somewhat trite and obvious conclusion that, as was to be expected, Italy, where the Renaissance originated, was also the country where modern science and mathematics began. In the sixteenth, and in part of the seventeenth century, she is supreme and then the scepter passes north, to Germany and England, France and Holland. As the various branches of knowledge became more intricate, after the end of the seventeenth century, no single country can be said to have distinguished itself in all of them for any long consecutive time. Let it be specifically remembered, likewise, that the particular country initiating certain new trends very frequently loses its commanding position in the subject under question within a few generations. Take, for example, modern chemistry. It began in England

and France in the last quarter of the eighteenth century and passed to Germany after the first quarter of the nineteenth. England lost her position in mathematics after the death of Newton and it passed, almost exclusively, to France in the eighteenth, although one of its very greatest figures, Lagrange, was an Italian. In the nineteenth century, Germany succeeded to the throne, although France never deteriorated greatly.

But if England did not distinguish herself in the eighteenth and part of the nineteenth century in the domain of pure mathematics, in the persons of Faraday and Clerk Maxwell, she completely dominated physics throughout most of the nineteenth century. In addition, by the generalizations of Darwin, she revolutionized biology and modern thought in the last century. At the end of that century, however, her work in biology had almost become nil and Darwinism gave place to Mendelianism. Chemistry, then, came into its own again there and physiology and physiological chemistry, two subjects in which England had hitherto never distinguished herself, became the best in Europe.

France, on the other hand, although maintaining her high standards in mathematics and physics during the nineteenth century, slumped markedly in chemistry and physiology toward the end of the century, although in Claude Bernard she had given the world one of the founders of the latter subject. In biology no one succeeded to the heritage of

Lamarck, Cuvier, and Geoffroy de Sainte-Hilaire and she was only superficially touched by Darwin and theory of evolution and Mendelism.

Germany, in the nineteenth century, distinguished herself by producing the greatest pure mathematician of his time Gauss, by equaling the record of France in physics and almost equaling that of England, and outdistancing everyone in chemistry and in zoology, botany, and physiology. Yet by the end of the century her supremacy was clearly passing. In zoology, botany, and physiology she had been overtaken and outdistanced by the United States, England, and, in part, by Italy, while her chemistry was visibly deteriorating. In pure mathematics she was still supreme. In mathematical physics, the fact that the relativity and the quantum theories had been worked out there gave her, for the time being, the dominant rôle in Europe. Yet she could only partially claim the glory for the formulation of the former generalization, because a Russian Jew and a German Jew had, in the main, accomplished this task. All indications pointed visibly to an approaching period of decline.

The bearing of all this on the problem of inherent racial and national characteristics is simple enough. A direct relation must be predicated between the intellectual performance of a people, their contact with the center from which the particular civilization radiated, their economic development, and the size of their population. Furthermore, in science and technology, progress and development take place, after a certain stage in their growth, by leaps and bounds and the particular individual who makes the specific contribution becomes of comparatively little importance. The record shows clearly that it would have been impossible to have foretold that the German Kepler was to be succeeded by the Danish nobleman Tycho Brahe, that he was to be followed by the Italian bourgeois Galileo, and the latter by the English gentleman Sir Isaac Newton. Similarly in the history of philosophy it would have been impossible to predict that the Portuguese-Dutch Jew Spinoza would have followed the Frenchman Descartes and that in succession there would then have been the Hanoverian Leibnitz, the Englishman Locke, the Scotchman Hume, and the Germans Kant and Hegel. Nor was there the slightest indication in the seventeenth and eighteenth centuries that Germany would develop a series of great historians and classical scholars in the nineteenth, or that the new revolution in mathematics would be due largely to a Russian and a Hungarian, and that it would be continued in the United States and Italy.

On any theory of special racial traits this is utterly unintelligible. It is intelligible only on the hypothesis that we are here in the presence of a single civilization and that, granted there be intercommunication between one group and another, the particular place in Europe or its colonial extensions where a great scientist will arise is unpredictable. In a population of, roughly speaking, 350,000,000 people, a given number of geniuses will exist and apply themselves to the solution of scientific and technological problems.

In terms of a generation, we may, at times, get the impression that ability is confined to a specific corner of the earth and to a specific people. When the time unit, however, is lengthened to two generations, doubt begins to arise; and when it is further lengthened to a century, our initial impression proves to be completely incorrect. Then it is borne in upon us that Europe is an indivisible cultural unit; that race, nationality, language and religion, and social status are secondary. The Catholic agnostic Laplace is found side by side with the Protestant agnostic Kant and the devout Protestant sectarian Faraday with the devout Catholic Pasteur; the history of the theory of relativity passes in continuous procession from the Russian Lobatchewsky to the Hungarian Bolyai, the German Riemann, the Russian Jew Minkowski, and the South German Jew Einstein; wireless telegraphy begins experimentally with the Englishman Faraday, is given mathematical expression by the Scotchman Clerk Maxwell, proved experimentally by the German Jew Hertz, and obtains practical application by the Italian Marconi.

Yet so naive and militantly irrational is the normal human mind, that, even in the face of these facts, the accredited dispensers of rationality, the university professors, would have us believe that the peoples who are momentarily dominant are genetically superior; and by dominant they mean, at bottom, economically dominant. Logically then we would have to assume that the Italians were genetically superior in the fifteenth and sixteenth centuries; England, France, and Holland in the seventeenth and eighteenth and England, Germany, France, and the United States in the nineteenth and twentieth. Since, however, the present German government contends that the German Jews were responsible for German economic prosperity in the nineteenth and twentieth centuries, we should have to substitute German Jews for Germans.

If, on the other hand, it is intellectual and not economic dominance that indicates genetic superiority, then we should be forced to the ridiculous conclusion that a people can, without any change in the selection of mates, develop a progressive genetic superiority, for instance, the Germans since the time of Goethe and the Jews since the beginning of the nineteenth century.

The case for the Jews on this assumption is amazingly good. They produced Disraeli, prime minister of England; Heinrich Heine, one of the greatest lyrical poets of all time; Karl Marx, the prophet of a new order, whose teachings have to a considerable extent been incorporated even into reactionary constitutions; Albert Einstein, who revolutionized our conception of the world; Henri Bergson, the most influential of modern philosophers, and Sigmund Freud who created a new psychology and a new method by which man could face himself. In addition, they were largely instrumental in building and completing our capitalistic system.

We should be further compelled to conclude that this miraculous genetic superiority can, within a short time, become quiescent, if indeed it be not transformed into downright inferiority. The racial theorists, not being able to deny this, are consequently in the awkward dilemma of being forced to give up, one after another, their outward criteria of genetic superiority. Intellectual achievement, economic dominance, military effectiveness, all have to go by the board, and only one criterion remains—a specific consciousness—a Germanic, French, English, Russian, Spanish, etc., soul. In other words, we have here a defeatist throwback, an attempt to regress to the type of mind which was dominant before the tremendous forward thrust which started with the Italian Renaissance.

It is one of the mockeries of fate that such a colossus of irrationality and such a palpably stuffed dragon as the thesis of racial superiority should have met with the favor of the very individuals who were helping to create the new art of thinking. In the main, however, they smelt the sawdust stuffing and succumbed only during a crisis, like the World War.

Apart from this one throwback into irrationality, the pan-European achievement has been an amazingly rational one and has worked consistently and steadily for the gradual democratization of the mind and of the heart. Religion, after all, is an aristocratic virtue, attainable by the few, and most of the worshippers are servants. There is no essential training of the heart involved. Saints and priests in the Middle Ages might spend their lives ameliorating the lot of the poor and the diseased but they sponsored no attempt to change conditions. The poor remained poor and the diseased, diseased. But the new science and the new technology brought with it the desire to experiment with man as well as with natural objects. If one could, in the domain of mathematics, visualize and formulate the laws governing probability and the infinite, why could it not be extended to that seemingly incalculable and recalcitrant aggregate of molecules and atoms, man? In the domain of science, far more forbidding problems had been attacked. The outward constitution of man had become increasingly well-known. The compound microscope, experimental embryology and Mendelian studies of heredity were depriving him of his privacy. From the chromosome to the full-grown embryo, all his movements were precisely catalogued and ticketed. Why not his mind and heart?

The opposition to such an extension of quantitative and qualitative intellectual curiosity was naturally tremendous. It was contended that human nature was human nature, which had fallen from its high estate by the wiles of a snake and the machinations of the eternal feminine, and since it had so fallen and since, in addition, an admirable home had been provided for man in the next world, why probe into the possibilities of this one? The clergy, it was contended, not to mention the lawyers and the politicians, were quite capable of manipulating and directing this pliable and temperamental human nature.

The scientists and philosophers of the late eighteenth century were not in the least devout, however, and beginning with Descartes they began the probe. By the time of Kant and Hegel, *i.e.*, by the first quarter of the nineteenth century, they had completed a fairly adequate philosophical analysis of man's mental life. At about the same time, particularly in England and Scotland, considerable strides had been made in the analysis of his feelings and motives. Yet, in spite of this, no attempt was made to alter anything about him. After all, these people were scientists and not men of affairs who were interested in improving mankind.

With the Industrial Revolution, beginning at the end of the eighteenth century, and the French Revolution, a new note appeared. Here, broadly speaking, were practical, tangible situations that had been brought about by the same forces that had engendered the new mind and all its wonders, and

103

they affected primarily man; affected him, in fact,
in such a way that a new type of human nature had
developed, the machine laborer and the proletarian.
Apparently then, human nature could change, and
apparently it changed in response to altered
conditions.

But the new economic order was to teach men
much more. The colonial expansions of England
and France brought them into contact with every
known race of the earth. Although these callous
soldiers and merchants insisted upon dominating
the native peoples economically, not even they
could fail to see that members of other races had
developed astounding civilizations and, what was
more, were very much like themselves. The first
answer of the whites to this realization was the
perfectly natural and intelligible one, *viz.*, that
since these people had a different skin color, spoke a
different language, and allowed themselves to be
conquered so easily, they must be inferior. Still,
inferior or not, contact with them did mean understanding them better and being influenced by as
well as influencing them.

Now it is one of the delightful aberrations of a
conqueror that he is so proud of those traits which
have enabled him to conquer other peoples that he
must needs pass them on to the conquered. In other
words, he must civilize them, no matter how much
it hurts. Thus the Orient was Europeanized during
the nineteenth century, thereby demonstrating what
104

the Europeans least desired, *viz.*, that the latter were their intellectual and even their technological equals.

The knowledge that human nature could change, that this came about through economic causes, and that white, yellow, black, red, and brown skins had very little to do with the qualities of mind and heart, broke down the last barriers to the final extension of the intellectual probing into the affairs of the human being. His nature was now to be gauged, the necessity for his living as he actually had lived for centuries critically examined, and he was to be apprised that his lot could be improved. This was simply the inevitable extension of the same type of reasoning into human affairs that scientists had been using for more than two centuries in their inquiries into nature. Social maladjustments were then simply equated with poor mechanisms in the technological world and regarded in the same light as the inadequately solved problems of the scientific world. But it meant more than a mere application of a scientific type of thinking to the problems of mankind; it also signified the application of a scientific type of feeling to these problems, a thinking of the heart.

This thinking of the heart showed itself specifically in the fact that religious minorities were permitted to participate actively in the life of the community. The most important of the minorities were unquestionably the Jews. The significant part that Jews have played during the nineteenth and twentieth centuries in the affairs of Europe seems, to many, so amazing that there has been an inclination to seek for its explanation in terms of superior ability. Attempts have even been made to account for this ability on the theory that they were a pure race. The racial question can be easily disposed of. They are one of the most mixed races in history.

The suddenness of their participation in the life of the communities in which they lived has likewise been somewhat exaggerated. This participation goes back at least two hundred and fifty years, although, of course, it had not been officially recognized so early. When at the beginning of the nineteenth century more or less official recognition was granted, much of the ability that had hitherto gone into their very rich local culture—literature, religious-philosophical works, and Talmudic exegesis—was immediately transferred to the more profitable subjects of science, mathematics, scholarship, and secular European literature. Since, however, a strong prejudice existed against them in the outside world and a specific antagonism against them within their own group, as being individuals who were endeavoring to break away from the old way of thinking, the particular individuals who actually succeeded in overcoming both types of prejudice were a highly selected group. Two other factors must be added; first, their business acumen and experience which in the new economic order, where business and trade were the earmarks of superiority, gave them

106

immediately both an assured station and a tremendous advantage over their new competitors and, second, their willingness to strike out on new paths. This latter can best be explained by a difference in cultural rhythm from those among whom they lived, and their greater liberty of action, since the fact that they were still somewhat outside the pale freed them from the taboos and restrictions of the majority. Thus they could embark on enterprises intellectual and practical, that were not strictly respectable; and when these subsequently became respectable, they naturally were given credit for originality and daring initiative. This enforced originality is one of the few privileges and advantages a minority possesses.

All these elements contributed strongly toward both the importance of the Jew's rôle in the nineteenth and twentieth centuries and the high estimate in which his abilities were held, just as they have also contributed largely to the development of antisemitism. This, in its turn, threw the Jews back upon themselves and induced them to resurrect the same type of nationalistic and racial myth as the Germans. In fact, the parallel between the history of the Germans and the Jews is often quite striking. Both of them were markedly maladjusted and both of them have had defeat and victory alternate with a maddening lack of regularity. But the Jews always had another tradition to fall back upon, so that they never became completely demoralized in defeat. Indeed it is this failure to become demoralized, when the peoples among whom they lived and whose language and culture they shared became so, that has led to an extreme bitterness and a violent increase of antisemitism, for no greater insult can befall a person than not to possess this essential element of a proper *esprit de corps*—of being rational when your neighbor is rational and irrational when he is irrational.

In this manner did the necessary corollary of the new mental revolution—the thinking of the heart—catapult an old virile minority out of its seclusion and force its members to take cognizance of the glorious new world. They thereupon took cognizance of it so efficiently that serious doubts arose among the kindly people who had invited them, nay, compelled them to participate, as to whether they had not better retire into seclusion again. And indeed, had it not been for the tremendous influence of a member of their race upon political and economic thought of the last three generations, and upon the extension of this very thinking of the heart, it is barely conceivable that they would have been compelled to return to the Talmud and its defensive mediaevalism. That Jew was Karl Marx.

That Marx was Jew has been somewhat wrongly stressed. He was not brought up as one and throughout his life showed no specific interest in Jews. Nor was it because he belonged to a submerged minority that he protested and became the proponent of a new order. Because he came from a Jewish environment, however, he escaped adherence to certain specific values of his non-Jewish surroundings; and because he rejected the Jewish background, he was liberated from these values as well. Thus he was doubly free, the prerequisite condition for the type of analysis of human society that he attempted. It had nothing to do with a Jewish mentality, a Jewish race, or a Jewish nationality. None of these exist in fact. It was simply the logical extension of the modern scientific mind to human problems.

This means, of course, the education of the heart and a new facing of human nature. Instead of explaining the latter as due to a fall from grace, a retreat from an unindividualized perfection, he sought to demonstrate, in modern fashion, that, whatever it may have been originally, today human nature had become the direct and immediate expression of social conditions. What mattered was not so much whether men and women were selfish, cruel, unfeeling, irrational, because of their original nature, as that they could not very well keep from being so under the conditions imposed by society. He had before him a special development of such conditions whose genesis was well-known.

The modern factory worker and proletarian had arisen barely a generation before his birth. The application of the scientific spirit of inquiry to this particular situation demonstrated definitely how easy it was for such attitudes and feelings as selfishness, jealousy, callousness, and cruelty to become mechanized, resulting in a tyranny and slavery, for producer as well as worker, of a hitherto unknown stringency and pitilessness. He argued quite correctly that only if these conditions changed would this specifically saturated selfishness and cruelty disappear, and he proceeded to work out the mechanism whereby society could change and what type of future society was both desirable and attainable. It was in no sense a Utopia, a lovely compensation myth, like that of Plato and Sir Thomas More. It was a vital amplification of the new art of thought.

The intense opposition to his analysis showed how well the powers in control realized the relentless logic of its implications and its tremendous danger to their whole structure. If not destroyed in time, this analysis, they realized, was likely to become generally accepted by both the mind and the heart. They consequently, acting precisely like the automata Marx contended they were, proceeded to buttress their entrenched position with all the means at their disposal. Knowing the uneducated human heart to perfection, they systematically appealed to its most unrelieved egotistical urges. Of these the easiest to approach was that based on common interests and traditions and a common speech, in short, nationalism. They attempted to identify these common interests with nationality and very adroitly made the argument fall both ways: nationality was endangered where the common interests were threatened and the common interests threatened where nationality was attacked.

In order to make the concept of nationality and race at all plausible, rationally and realistically, it was imperative that no large numbers of any particular race or nationality be taken as representative, for then the divergences and contradictions would be too apparent. Thus there arose a concept of race and nationality built up by the process of the elimination of one trait after another and when the image was complete it was almost perfect of its kind. Who indeed would not wish to be such an Englishman, such a Frenchman, such a Jew, such a German! True, this individual no longer existed, for time and corruption deal harshly with all that is good and true. Yet once he had existed, and who knows but that by dint of hard labor and by the extension of the home markets one could approximate to him again! In any case, such a faith was more ennobling and worthy of the human heart than this materialistic stressing of envy and hatred which Marx had introduced.

This, then, is the third element that enters into the texture of the nationalistic and racial myth— the attempt to divert attention from the logical inferences inherent in any analysis of society, by appealing to the glorified and heroic image each individual makes of himself.

Yet even this strong combination—the myth of a Golden Age, the tradesman's slogans, and the hero image—was powerless to stem the encroaching rationalizing of the heart. The world had to be seen as it was and man had to be seen as his world made him. If human nature, as constituted today, could not endure the anguish of beholding such a world, it would either itself have to change or transform the world into a more palatable sight. The second alternative seemed infinitely easier to Marx and the Marxists. Human nature would respond, they felt, and become ameliorated as soon as the social conditions did. Now this was rank optimism and the opponents of socialism seized upon it as the best demonstration of the wholly Utopian nature of the theory. The same people who had constructed the godlike images of race and nationality protested in the same breath that man was naturally a bandit and that his desire to obtain something for nothing, as well as to take what belonged to his neighbor, was so great and of so compulsive a nature that he would inevitably break up all such approximations to paradise, just as he had destroyed the first one. They counseled poor distracted and erring man to keep his dreams pure and undefiled, and to project them either into the past or the very distant future.

It was inevitable, however, that a time would come when some one would undertake to pose once more the question of whether human nature itself could change. Certain pathological changes the world had always known, and it is not strange that it was from the students of such cases that the first inquiry into this subject came. Such studies were naturally looked upon askance, but by the end of the nineteenth century there was an adequate number of scientists, particularly in Germany and France, sufficiently withdrawn from the majority of their cultural taboos to brave the criticism and antagonism aroused by their probing too deeply into such a problem. From abnormal man it was only natural to turn to normal man and this is what Sigmund Freud attempted in psychoanalysis.

The storm that greeted his first researches most of us remember. He was denounced and vilified as a conscienceless Jew, bent upon destroying the Holy of Holies, who delighted in wallowing in filth and obscenity. And what, precisely, had he done? Simply pushed a critical and essentially humanitarian inquiry into the thoughts and emotions of human beings as far as it could go. Many of the facts he unearthed, physicians, particularly psychiatrists, had always known. What distinguished Freud from all his predecessors and makes him stand alone is that he insisted that, if man recognized honestly and fearlessly the nature of his motives and actions as well as the nature of their genesis, he could become, as it were, a new man and a more desirable member of society. In other words, he taught that all the numerous

113

cases of maladjustment were due primarily to problems arising out of the struggle of the individual with the specific social environment in which he found himself placed and to which he had to conform. In masterly fashion he taught man to face himself, to be properly frightened, to be thoroughly ashamed, and then slowly to understand himself in a manner utterly new and refreshing. Some solace he might possibly have found in the fact that great and small, rich and poor, black and white and yellow, long-heads and round-heads, all alike, when prodded, disclosed the same internal psychic fauna and flora.

From the investigations of the psychoanalysts it was clearly apparent that man, everywhere, was basically and fundamentally similar and that his idiosyncracies, his strange illusions, his queernesses were all due to explicable distortions, that these distortions were more or less brought about by special aspects of civilization itself, and that they varied from culture to culture. Particularly revealing was the analysis of the elements involved in all such constructions as nation and race.

Thus from another source were we informed of the wholly irrational origin of these concepts. Not only was their genesis given, but a reasonable explanation offered of why they persist and what measures must be taken by each individual to prevent their persistence. While psychoanalysts were, however, not concerned with theories of society as such and attempted to make no judgments here, they were, nevertheless, vitally concerned with pointing out what was true and what was illusion, as well as the deleterious effects that follow from confusing the two. To point out, however, that national and racial pretensions are illusions and partake of the nature of adolescent myths is the only condemnation a normally thinking man can demand.

The larger and assuredly more fundamental question of the reasons for the persistence of such myths, *viz.*, their usefulness in economic exploitation, the psychoanalysts and other critics of these myths do not, of course, touch, and part of their analysis is vitiated by this neglect. How dangerous this neglect on the part of the very people who recognize the true constituents of these gaudy structures can become is shown by the eugenists who, in the interests of these illusions, are today advocating sterilization of the "unfit."

But sterilization of the unfit implies the existence of a theory of desirable traits that should be encouraged. What are they? Obviously they will depend upon the so-called ideals of the particular group in power. Hitler's Germany will sterilize those who by their utterances indicate that they are not true Aryans. If we follow Herr Helmuth Nicolai, Minister of Justice, the present authorities in Germany will determine this by the Teutonic feeling inherent in them. Yet, even at best, the final judges will be physicians and lawyers. But when, precisely, did physicians and lawyers attain to this supreme wisdom? We know that in the actual practice of their professions they are frequently swayed by wholly subjective evaluations and that they are primarily and fundamentally upholders of an existing order of things. They desire society to be ill and maladjusted so that they can apply their pills and palliatives. That is, after all, how they live. They would consequently merely be agents of the powers in control, have society breed for those virtues admirable in a capitalistic order. It is here that they would again utilize the racial myth, arguing, apparently, on the supposition that the multiplication of two illusions gives one full-fledged reality.

In the United States, of late, many tears have been shed over the dying-out of the good old New England families. Salem is being conquered by the Pole and Cabotinsky has become Cabot. Yet I am under the impression that, in the dim and remote past, Cabot itself had been abbreviated from Caboto and that the original progenitor was not even a Nordic. Apparently we are to breed for the chromosomes that enabled the founders of the republic to conquer a rock-bound coast, expand the American frontier, and engage in the slave traffic. But the rock-bound coast has been conquered; the frontier is gone. To breed for these traits, if they are to function, would expose us to the suspicion of having imperialistic designs and, if they are not to function, would inevitably lead to neuroses if not psychoses.

If the eugenists are so thoroughly wrought up about the maintenance of a special group within the white race itself, it is not difficult to realize how frantic they become about the advisability of race intermixture. The race problem is somewhat easier to handle where individual groups within an alien race have attained cultural eminence, as in the case of the Chinese and Japanese. There the argument is frankly based upon what they would contend is the natural incompatibility of Mongolians and whites to live together in harmony and to advantage. Since the Mongolians have manifestly achieved great civilizations and Japan is, at present, even imitating the standard white values of culture with Frankensteinian adroitness and terrifying cunning, the charge of inherent inferiority is impossible. We must, therefore, infer that a difference in skin color and in the conformation of the eyelid is responsible for this incompatibility.

The charge of inferiority can, however, be made against the Negro race, they insist. It is true that the only difference between the Mongolian and the Negro is that of skin color. But, after all, yellow is closer to white than black, and the Negro never developed a civilization comparable to that of the Chinese or Japanese. The fact that here in America, under unusually adverse conditions, he

117

absorbed European culture so completely that, within three hundred years of his enforced landing, he was able to produce an essentially original literature and music, seems to be beside the point. They have forgotten that it took Northern Europe, under infinitely more favorable conditions, at least twice as long to absorb Graeco-Roman civilization and do anything with it.

But, granted that certain traits are desirable, how can we, if society, more especially our present economic order, dictates our behavior, know what individuals possess these traits and how they can be bred? The answer is simple: there is no way. One of the foremost eugenists in America, H. J. Muller, has put the matter convincingly and authoritatively as follows:

. . . Individual economic considerations rather than considerations of the genetic worth of the future generations must in the main govern human reproduction, in so far as the latter is voluntary at all, and eugenics must remain an idle dream. . . . The apologists [for our present system] have put forward the naive doctrine that the economically dominant classes, races and individuals are genetically superior. Such scientific evidence as is available fails to support this contention. . . . On theoretical grounds, in fact, there is at least as much reason for supposing that the dominant classes represent a selection of socially inferior, as of socially superior genetic material. . . .

In our economic system . . . the ideal set of characteristics, which most present-day eugenists and the population at large would set up as a eugenic goal, is far from the type which would be considered most desirable in a well-ordered society.[1]

[1] *The Scientific Monthly*, pp. 46–47, July, 1933.

It is thus unadulterated dishonesty if the inaugurators of the Third Reich pretend that they have suddenly become unduly exercised about the possibility of the hopelessly insane or the diseased propagating their kind to the detriment of society. Yet the amazing crudity of their utterances serves an admirable purpose, for it allows us to visualize concretely the extent to which a dying order of society is willing to go in order to save itself and the unrelieved stupidity and cruelty to which a racial and nationalistic myth can be pushed.

Were the eugenists really serious in their avowed intention of improving the human race, they would try to isolate and determine those cultural chromosomes that make for kindness and understanding, and, above all, they would try to see to it that they themselves raise a race of successors who possess enough acumen to discriminate between fiction and fact, between illusion and reality, and between obvious humbug and clarified vision.

But there is some consolation to be derived, even from all this riotous extravagance and palpable irrationality. It is an indication that the art of thought is being perfected, the realm of the dark and hidden illumined; that we are even prepared to deprive man of the last refuge to which he is wont to retire in time of stress—the secret places of the soul. Justly so, for the time being, at least. For these secret places of the soul are frequently the breeding places of myth and illusion. It is from some neglected corner of the soul that we are attacked in our many irrational moments, attacked and overwhelmed by verbalized yearnings and by a hazy nostalgia that is probably as old as the trauma of birth. Even so immense an intuition and understanding as that of Goethe's was thus overwhelmed when he said:

> Das Schaudern ist der Menschheit bestes Teil.
> Wie auch die Welt ihm das Gefühl verteuere
> Ergriffen fühlt er tief das Ungeheuere.[2]

It is precisely against this, however, that man must guard himself, for the shudder of awe attaches itself to myriads of phantasms and gives them a vital, even if false and dangerous, reality. Race and nationality are so enveloped. Only a relentless application and deepening of the art of thought and the thinking of the heart as envisaged by Karl Marx and Sigmund Freud can ward off its insidious threat. The Germans and the Jews may well be proud of them.

[2] It is almost impossible to translate this. However, I offer the following: "The shudder of awe is the best part of man. Even if the world and experience endear his feelings to him hundredfold, still it is only the tremendous, the terrifying immense, which seizes him and possesses him to his very depths."

CHAPTER VI

THE CONFEDERATION OF THE WORLD

Man, in common with our household pets, has always been described as a domesticated animal. Yet all biologists and anthropologists are agreed that domestication implies the change from a wild to a tame stage and an agency to bring about the transformation. For animals like the cat and the dog man performed this task. But who performed it for man? Simple and fundamental as the question is, there is no adequate answer. Yet we may surmise that the tamer originally was the human mind, that it took place without design or purpose, and that even today the vestiges of this accidental taming are still with us. We may further surmise that within a comparatively short time after he emerged as man he subjected himself to the control of societies which he had himself organized, and that thereafter the mind was aided in its self-imposed task by these societies themselves. Thereupon there must have sprung up that three-fold strife which has characterized the history of man ever since—the strife of the mind with the body, of society with the mind, and of the body with the body. The first gave us dreams and ethics, the second gave us conservatives and radicals, and the third gave us war.

Thus, in the dim fog of the past, man started with three handicaps. From dreams and ethics he derived his fondness for illusion; from the struggle of the conservatives with the radicals, his unwillingness to progress; and from the buffeting of body against body, his mania for extolling physical prowess. With such an array of enemies against it, the mind was hard pressed and responded in an unfortunate even if intelligible manner: it bestowed validity upon illusion, gave consecration to the past, and insisted that war was but an idealization of the instinct of pugnacity and that the instinct of pugnacity was inherent in man. Possibly there was no other alternative. Yet, carefully considered, this stamp of approval constituted a surrender on the part of the mind, a retreat to the oldest part of his physical make-up. It is not true that illusion is necessary, that the past need be consecrated, and that man is naturally pugnacious. For one hundred thousand years now, we have suffered from this makeshift hypothesis, whose only justification is that under the circumstances it was both pardonable and explicable.

Yet, though the mind might err, with the mind man began, and through it he must conquer. Even a mystic and anti-intellectual like St. John realized that the mind is the light that shineth in the darkness and that the darkness apprehended it not. Slowly, through the ages, the mind was to continue in its self-imposed task of disproving these initial and erroneous approximations toward an explanation of man's disharmony with himself, with society, and with others, and slowly man was to arrive at some justification for his faith that this strife could cease, that it was a phase of his existence, not its essence. For thousands of years he sought to put off the pain and travail which he rightly sensed was necessary for his upward struggle by postponing the attainment of this harmony to another world, after death. But it is here in this world that harmony must be attained and it can never be a God-bestowed gift. Before this could be accomplished, however, the external world had to be conquered, analyzed, and made tributary.

The stages of that conquest, as well as the gradual encroachment of the mind upon the domain of man's animal manifestations, have been outlined in the preceding chapters. We have pointed out the milestones in that conquest and that growth, from Paleolithic and Neolithic times to the invention of writing, the Greeks, the Renaissance, modern

123

science and the machine, and the new economic order that came in the wake of the new art of thought, partly dictated by it, partly dictating it. We have seen how, as soon as the technique of thought attained its new perfection after the Renaissance, man turned his analysis successively upon the external world, the mind of man, the economic and social conditions of existence, and, finally, upon human nature itself.

The cultural detritus that had accumulated, however, was enormous. Myths and illusions had been crystallized and had become so inextricably interwoven with the fundamental realities and with practical activities that not merely were they difficult to expose, they were even difficult, at times, to discern and, when they were seen, even brave men were unwilling to touch them. Tender hopes and vibrant ideals had been built around them; beautiful and glorious literatures nestled lovingly in their embrace. It seemed to betoken heartlessness and insensitiveness to disentangle them from the realities with which they had for so many generations been connected, and to show that the myths were devoid of reality and the reality of myths.

As both thus stood out in their nakedness, they appeared uninviting, sordid, and materialistic. It was but natural to assume that the people who gave their lives to such a task were themselves uninviting, materialistic, and sordid, that the beauty of existence had escaped them. When these mate-

124

rialists protested that, on the contrary, they were attempting to establish a new order for all those who had been cruelly deprived of even the opportunity to look upon this beauty, not to mention the necessary training for enjoying it, they were called fools and utopians.

Since the beginning of the world, however, every new measure, every new proposal has been so designated. Doubtless nature made the same comment when the human mind first undertook to domesticate that brazen savage man. In the course of time, initiators learned that to be called a fool and a utopian was the first stage of recognition. What they did not learn was how easy it was for their new ideas and reforms to become entangled in weeds, and the devious ways in which the dead hand of the past and the dead hand of the living could deprive them of their victory.

By the middle of the nineteenth century, however, even the seemingly impregnable fortress that these two forces of culture had erected seemed about to totter. The mind had, at last, penetrated the heart. The darkness that apprehended not undertook one last sally and that sally can be expressed in two words: racialism and nationalism. The very fact that it was necessary to fall back upon that glorified illusion and myth which is race and the heroic manipulation of the ego which is nationality showed how desperate the need was. That did not destroy its efficiency, however. All the momentum of a well-organized economic system was thrown into the struggle, which now began and which ended in the World War. The sign under which they fought was race and nationality; that under which the Treaty of Versailles signed, race and nationality; and that under which Hitler's Third Reich was reared, race and nationality. And today, barely sixteen years after the Armistice, what is the symbol with which white Europe and America threatens Japan and with which Japan threatens the rest of the world? Race and nationality.

We have shown out of what strands the thin garment of race and nationality was woven. Within the last hundred years it has assuredly become clear to all thinking hearts why the strangle hold of these two virile specters persists, as well as their purpose. The events, internal and external, which have brought about this recognition and realization are not transient episodes or intellectual and emotional vagaries. They represent a logical and resistless development in which all peoples and all races have participated, some more definitely at one time, some more definitely at another. They are now pressing forward toward their ultimate solution and that solution itself will again test the hold these symbols possess. As in the past, so in the future the initiative for this next thrust will come from specific peoples, who through sheer accident, and not through inherent ability, are best prepared and qualified to be in the vanguard and to bear the brunt. There can be little doubt that those nations not participating at the outset, will be inclined to resent the leadership which circumstances have forced upon the others and that, again, the cry will be raised, "O dear fatherland, sweet mother tongue, the foe is at your door!"

While it is too much to hope that man will not, for the time being, at least, succumb to this call, still the indications are that it will not be for long and that the penetrating analyses of Karl Marx and Sigmund Freud will have done their work— that of stripping social and personal myths of their efficacy by forcing them to stand forth in all their undress, and that of steeling the mind and heart to look upon them calmly and understandingly.

That victory depends upon the possession of power, that force and bloodshed, unfairness and cruelty may be necessary is evident. This is extremely unfortunate as the intellectuals and the artists, those who happen to possess the gift for articulating the nature of this struggle and analyzing men and events know very well. They are, generally, the very individuals who abhor and detest both lust for power and violence. They cannot work or properly function in such an atmosphere. But it is insincere twaddle and sheer hypocrisy for the leaders and supporters of our present economic system to protest against the seizure of power and the attendant destruction of opponents when this occurs in pursuance of aims and purposes antagonistic to their own. For they necessarily live by violence, maintain their position by violence, and can, probably, only be dispossessed by violence. Being men of great acumen and possessing a pitiless knowledge of reality, surely they must know this.

In the coming struggle for power, the leaders in the revolt will unquestionably have to be those countries which, through chance, possess three advantages: a past that has been completely discarded, the absence of hereditary social distinctions, and a living and intimate acquaintance with members of another race. That is why they must be the Russians, the Americans, and the Jews.

Leaving the Jews aside for a moment, it might be instructive merely to point out the extent of the territory embraced by Russia, Siberia, and the two Americas. It is literally half the world and includes every known modern race. Moreover, it contains peoples in all stages of economic development and even in all degrees of physical miscegenation. In no single one of the main countries of this area is one single language spoken, even though the official language is definitely fixed and the unofficial languages are rapidly disappearing. The conditions for a very favorable reception to racial and nationalistic claims and pretensions should, on the face of it, hardly be very good. And, in fact, racial theories were never seriously promulgated in any one of these countries, with the exception of the United States, during the last two generations.

In the United States the early development of capitalism was fairly exclusively in the hands of the descendants of the early English immigrants and newcomers completely dominated by them, and only when their control was threatened was the race issue raised. Into Latin America the capitalistic system had barely penetrated and then only as an overflow from the United States. Since, in addition, race mixture was there the order of the day, a deification of the white race was quite impossible. A certain kind of nationalism, however, did develop. But this was manifestly simply an extravagant form of the crudest and most infantile provincialism. The unfortunate economic dependence of these countries upon the United States, which they quite correctly called the colossus of the north, has kept them in this condition for the last generation. Russia escaped true nationalism, except for an ineffective intellectual type, for reasons that are so well known that one need not dwell upon them. Any insistence upon racial purity was, of course, out of the question.

All these peoples then are magnificently prepared for that form of mutual understanding and tolerance which lies at the basis of all true internationalism. They have all, likewise, in one fashion or another, despite considerable lip service to a mother country or, as in the case of Russia before the revolution, to a pan-Slavism, broken fundamentally with the past, done away with hereditary social distinctions,

129

and, finally, have a living and intimate acquaintance with members of another race.

The Jews form a group by themselves. Their ancient insistence upon regarding themselves as a pure race, with a specific mentality and even a particular mission to perform, has been very properly relegated to the realm of religion. In spite of the separatistic tendencies of that core which holds steadfastly to hoary dogmas and customs that have no relation to the modern world of reality, they must, from the very essence of their history, be sympathetic to every form of internationalism. For them, at this late date, to embark on a nationalistic enterprise is a contradiction in terms and can be properly understood only as the desperate remedy of a persecuted and hard-pressed minority in an untenable situation, and possibly as an indication of how they too can succumb to myths. They are clearly divided into three groups: the religious separatists, those who participate actively in the life around them and still profess a tenuous yet persistent allegiance to their specific past, and the small but important group who have broken with the specific culture around them and with the specific past of their own people. It is because of these three elements in their culture that they have been charged with being, at one and the same time, an oriental and alien minority, with having a double loyalty, and with being the disrupters of the peace, *i.e.*, having no loyalty at

130

all. And it is precisely because of these three component elements that they are so admirably fitted for participating in new economic programs and in internationalism.

Thus the conditions that make these three groups —the Russians, the Americans, and the Jews—such fertile soil for future experiments, looking toward the framing of a new and ordered society, are purely historical and in no way indicate inherent racial fitness for this particular task, a fact that it might be well for future historians to remember, assuming that future historians are like many of those of today. Yet favorable conditions in themselves do not suffice. They have existed in the past without leading to any but temporary successes. What warrant have we for believing, therefore, that we are arrived at a turning point in human history? The answer is two contemporary events: the constructive realism of the Russian experiment and the destructive romanticism of Hitler's Third Reich.

The Russian experiment, whatever be our attitude to it, is the first real attempt to apply the principles that Marx enunciated and in the manner advocated, which was by the seizure of power. The Russian socialists had, of course, learned from the experience of German and French socialism how easy it was for sincere radicals to succumb to the fleshpots of compromise. A roseate Victorian atmosphere hung about the latter. Men were supposed, on the whole, to be reasonable and rational. Toleration was in the air. But tolerance, however desirable it may seem, is at bottom a luxury, and a seductive one at that. It presupposes a world of philosophers, sages, and gentlemen, and Europe between 1870 and 1914 was obviously a world of shopkeepers, proletarians, and peasants, who had neither time nor patience with what they quite rightly regarded as the well-bred gesture of a leisure class. Yet just because it was the definite insignia of a well-bred gentleman, it was naturally adopted by the rising radical political parties. If radicalism was a sign of political progress, why, *noblesse oblige*, like gentlemen shall we behave! Thus the German and French socialists paid for their good manners by giving up their principles and surrendering their influence. Power they never possessed.

The Bolsheviks could thus gain insight from this bitter experience. They seized the power and proceeded to abolish tolerance, on the correct theory that the latter was a luxury that could well be postponed to later times. They also demonstrated that they knew why they had seized power and what was to be done with it; that they had properly observed the captains of industry and learned the key to their success. The crucial question was whether they could use it realistically and scientifically, for only then should we discover the extent to which the new art of thought and the thinking of the heart had become instruments for social amelioration and social progress. That is precisely what, they feel, they have done. Not only did they plan intelligently and force these plans to completion with almost cynical ruthlessness, but they, at the same time, attacked the two myths that had led to so much distortion and bloodshed—racialism and nationalism. The one sin against the Holy Ghost was to express allegiance to these two illusions. And this in the land of the Czarist pogroms!

To teach the human heart to think was more difficult, especially in a land of peasants. The methods often had to be direct and reminiscent of Sunday school instruction. Thus, in a meeting of a suburban village Soviet, a peasant woman objected to an item in the taxes to provide shoes for needy children. "Why should I give money and get nothing for it in return?" she said. Whereupon the chairman assured her, "To give and get nothing for it in return, that you must learn. That is socialism."

The fundamental trait of the founders of socialism was this combination of "a capacity for critical analysis and philosophical generalization with emotional reaction to human values, and a willingness to sacrifice comfort and risk liberty for them. To these, in the decisive historical moment, Lenin added the courage and will to translate dialectical judgment into action."[1]

[1] WARD, H. F., *In Place of Profit*, p. 443, 1933.

133

Our warrant, then, for regarding the present era as a turning point in human history is this fact: that an experiment is being tried rationally, realistically, and with an honest and vigorous application of a carefully thought-out plan where nothing has been neglected. Human nature is recognized for what it is. The leaders have mapped out precisely what appetites, habits, prejudices, and opinions it is necessary to change in order to realize their social ideal and they know equally well how many years must be required to remake the worker and the peasant. They have clearly visualized all the steps necessary for this transformation and all the dangers. Thus in the transition between capitalism and socialism there must, unquestionably, they feel, be a partial return to primitive democracy. Of the great danger of falling into bureaucracy with its attendant deadly routine they are well aware. To keep man from falling into the bondage of the forms he has himself created, new ideas and new blood are being continually infused into the organization and a goal proclaimed that leads him from change to change.

H. F. Ward, in the work just quoted has significantly summed up the essence of their theory and practice as follows:

It is upon the dynamic nature of their social ideal as well as upon the increasing participation of the population in all forms of administration, that the communists rely to enable them to break the historic rule that all revolutionary movements

134

crystallize into authoritative institutions which forbid change. There is another penalty of age, for parties as well as for men. It is the tendency to be content, with winning one fight. . . . The Machine Age, because of its laboratory concern with the immediate, tends to withdraw men's eyes from the distant goal for human living. The only means of escape from these disastrous tendencies is the vision of a moving goal, whose pursuit requires a continuous revolutionary process in human nature. The communist idea affirms the former, its basic philosophy requires the latter. . . . Their ideal is in terms of values that are capable of infinite development and require continuous struggle. They do no permit themselves to regard any social forms they are now developing as final. The only thing they are attempting to fix beyond the power of change is the general direction of advance.[2]

Surely this type of consciousness, whether or not we agree with the specific form it has taken in Russia, is the direct outcome of that progress in the art of thought which began in the Renaissance, and surely it is the best protection against myths.

Opposed to this constructive realism, this superior consciousness, we have the realistic and destructive romanticism of the Third Reich, which is completely steeped in the unconscious. The justification for our contention that it betokens the end of a system as definitely as does the Russian experiment lies in the fact that such putrefaction is always the harbinger of the imminence of dissolution. There is not a single one of its injunctions and precepts that is not palpably and ludicrously wrong. There

[2] *Ibid.*, p. 390.

never was an Aryan race; the Germans are not, to any extent, Nordic; the old system of law in which they have taken refuge for their new code was not to any appreciable degree Germanic; the small businessman class which they wish to resurrect and reenforce is unmistakably dead, and so on, *ad infinitum*. This atmosphere of the madhouse cannot possibly represent the mood of 65,000,000 people who have always been known for their middle-of-the-road sanity; it cannot represent the permanent mood of madmen. The only conceivable interpretation is that this semblance of madness, this intensification of that old Teutonic virtue, the berserker rage, conceals something else—the last wild attempt to stave off the impending transformation of an economic system. That it should assume such crude forms is the most significant indication of its transitoriness and its inherent weakness. Actually, having regard for their economic development and for their habits of mind and thought, it would be easier to impose a communistic order upon the Germans than upon any other major civilization in the world. That possibly is the reason for the present terror and that possibly will account, in part, for the manifest madness of the leaders of the Third Reich.

Myths thrive in such an atmosphere and are at a premium, particularly those myths which are fiendish, fiendish for those who believe in them and for those who suffer from them. Yet even men of seeming integrity and penetration succumb. When the day for alibis arrives, how, then, will he appear in retrospect, Altmeister Gerhardt Hauptmann, with his mock-heroic affirmation of the Third Reich, *Ich sage Ja* (*I do affirm*)?

In the United States, despite our anarchy, our rugged individualism, and our tolerance, which has become practically identical with loss of values, the conditions for a constellation favorable and sympathetic to a cooperative state are definitely promising. This may seem a hopelessly optimistic statement in view of the recent epidemic of lynchings and the ease with which, in the past, prejudices have crystallized into mob activities. But, at bottom, American history has made for realism. Apart from the South, American romanticism has always been skin deep and symbolism has never existed. Democratic individualism possesses a comparatively small orbit and that orbit has been covered so completely and so frequently that the tracks are completely worn out. It requires no great prophetic insight to realize not only that a new orbit must be found but that this orbit cannot be a continuation of the old one. The rigidity of our administrative units may interpose—unquestionably will interpose—vicious obstacles to such a revolution. But rigidity is often far more pliable than elasticity.

Clearly the old myths race and nationality have no vitality here and the secondary myth of rugged individualism is, for the time being, under eclipse.

137

In spite of all prejudices against other races, Negro and Mongolian, we do know them in a manner no other white race can. We do not have to go to our colonies to meet them. They are in our very midst, part and parcel of our culture, possessing the same allegiance, the same customs, and the same language as ourselves. Our immediate neighbors and colleagues, in Mexico, Central America, Cuba, and South America, with whom we are in intimate relation and with whom in the future our intimacy must increase, are a mixed people. Race prejudice, consequently, can never be much more than an economic excuse; it cannot correspond to a true intellectual or even emotional reality, nor can the myths developed in connection with these superficial racial prejudices ever acquire more than temporary virulence. What is, perhaps, more fundamental: they can never be mistaken for anything except myths.

The struggle for power in the United States, consequently, is a purely economic one that has, fortunately, within recent times been deprived of all its ornamental trappings. It is seen realistically, exactly for what it is. The measures of the present administration make clear that even necessarily capitalistic administrators realize that the only problem confronting them is how the new reorganization is to come about, the precise measures and the time required for putting it into effect. Taking a leaf from the Russians, they seem to be interested not so much in prophesying what forms the new movement shall assume as *in fixing beyond the power of change the general direction it is to go.* In the last analysis, of course, phrases and plans and good-will can mean nothing. Everything will depend upon who seizes power. Yet the general significance of the new trend is clear enough: the new interpenetration of an intelligent heart by a properly functioning mind that has reached even the high places of the most predatory form of the capitalistic system we know.

However, it is not a question of labels with which mankind is concerned today, nor is it a question of whether a new order will arise today or tomorrow. The essential fact is that the whole social system that developed toward the end of the eighteenth century, and the whole system of thought and emotions associated with it, is irrevocably dead, and that the general outlines of the new order which is to replace it are fairly well foreshadowed in every major contemporary civilization, whether it regard itself as reactionary or revolutionary. Even that hideous regression into an imaginary and unintegrated past, the present Third Reich, has to parade in slogans belonging to that coming order. A tyrannous inevitability dictates its appearance, for the very same causes that brought about modern capitalism have also destroyed it and these very same forces are now inaugurating the new cooperative state. Such a state must be based upon a world that has broken with its past, that is cosmopolitan in the broadest sense of the term, and for that reason Russia, the United States, and the Jews must be in the vanguard of the peoples who are to forge this commonwealth.

The resistance to this transformation of society, where it is not due to easily understandable egotistical motives, comes from a clear misreading of the past, due to the obsessive and irrational hold daily habits of the mind and of the heart have upon us. But there are no inherent habits of the mind and heart of civilized man. They are all specifically determined by the former generation, and it will be as easy to have the habits and outlook that the proponents of the new order demand, then, as it is to have our present ones, today. It is to that new interlocking of the mind with the heart and of the heart with the mind, beginning specifically in the seventeenth century and receiving its best articulate expression in such minds as Marx and Lenin, Freud and Jung, that we must ascribe this realization.

We need not worry about the glories of the past ever being forgotten or not receiving their due recognition. The past has always taken care of itself with meticulous and automatic regularity. This is precisely what we have at last been taught to guard against—the meticulous and automatic regularity with which the past repeats itself. The society of tomorrow intends to regulate how much of this is to be incorporated into the present. We simply cannot trust the past. Is not Hitler the incarnation of what an uncontrolled past will do, and the atrocities committed in the name of the myth of nationalism, of the myth of rugged individualism, and the myth of racial superiority?

A part of the past we can cherish and incorporate into the present—that we know; just as that all nations and races have contributed to its formation. For the moment, however, all but the scientific heritage will have to abide its time. The coming society will be concerned—regrettably it must be said—primarily with the answer the past has given to one question, one which the great German Goethe has put into the mouth of Prometheus in his defiance of the Greek incarnation of the past, the god Zeus:

> Hast du die Schmerzen gelindert
> Je des Beladenen?
> Hast du die Thränen gestillet
> Je des Geängsteten?[3]

[3] Didst thou ever assuage the suffering of the oppressed?
Didst thou ever dry the tears of the frightened and terrorized?